Machine Learning for Beginners

Absolute Beginners Guide,
Learn Machine Learning and
Artificial Intelligence from Scratch

Chris Sebastian

Table of Contents

Introduction 4

Chapter 1: History of Machine Learning 7

Chapter 2: Theories of Machine Learning 14

Chapter 3: Approaches to Machine Learning 20

    Philosophies of Machine Learning 21

    Supervised and Semi-supervised Learning Algorithms 27

    Unsupervised Learning Algorithms..................... 29

    Reinforcement Learning 31

Chapter 4: Machine Learning and Artificial Intelligence 33

Chapter 5: Machine Learning and Neural Networks 37

    Feedforward Neural Networks............................. 39

    Recurrent Neural Networks 41

    Backpropagation.. 42

Chapter 6: Machine Learning and Big Data 44

Chapter 7: Machine Learning and Regression 53

Chapter 8: Machine Learning and the Cloud 56

    Benefits of Cloud-Based Machine Learning 61

Chapter 9: Machine Learning and the Internet of Things (IoT)... 64

- Consumer Applications 66
- Commercial Applications 70
- Industrial Applications 76
- Infrastructure Applications 81
- Trends in IoT 87

Chapter 10: Machine Learning and Robotics 99
- Examples of Industrial Robots and Machine Learning 104

Chapter 11: Machine Learning and Swarm Intelligence 106
- Swarm Behavior 107
- Applications of Swarm Intelligence 108

Chapter 12: Machine Learning Models 113

Chapter 13: Applications of Machine Learning 120

Chapter 14: Programming and (Free) Datasets 131
- Data Sets 132
- Online Machine Learning Resources 135

Chapter 15: Limitations of Machine Learning 137
- The Philosophical Objections: Jobs, Evil, and Taking Over the World 147

Chapter 16: Machine Learning and the Future 154

Conclusion 162

Introduction

Perhaps nothing human beings ever do will have as much impact on their future as artificial intelligence. It is a hidden revolution, though, quietly taking place all around us without most people even being aware it is happening. We speak to our phones and they speak back. We rely on an electronic map to not only guide us to a location but to get us there using the quickest route and avoiding traffic congestion. From IT incursion detection to medical diagnosis, the areas where Machine Learning is improving our lives are many and growing every day.

Machine Learning is based in mathematics, specifically statistics. It is a probabilistic discipline that began in the 1950s. Despite initial enthusiasm, research and development in Machine Learning languished for over 30 years, suffering from twin ills of a lack of data to work with and computers that were too slow to effectively work with what data they had.

It is no accident Machine Learning is coming into its own over the last 10 years. Until we began creating and storing massive amounts of data about our world, Machine Learning was mostly an idea in the minds of statisticians. And until computers reached a level of speed and power where these massive data sets could be ingested in a reasonable amount of time, the revolution couldn't happen. But as we digitize information about our world and ourselves, and computers continue to increase in speed and capacity exponentially, the ability for Machine Learning to learn from our data grows in depth and accuracy. Looking to the future, we can see only more and more data collection about our world, faster computer chips and data transfer, and more avenues for Machine Learning to develop in, to grow and learn, and to serve humanity.

The following chapters in this book will chart the development of Machine Learning, from its theoretical history through the different approaches being used today, to the future that Machine Learning will, at least in part, be responsible for creating. Along the way, we will discover some of the limitations of Machine Learning, as well as possible dangers this new powerful form of computer thinking may pose.

There are plenty of books on this subject on the market, so thanks again for choosing this one! Every effort was made to ensure it is full of as much useful information as possible. Please enjoy!

Chapter 1:

History of Machine Learning

The history of Machine Learning begins with the history of computing. And this history began before computers were even invented. The function of computers is actually math, in particular, boolean logic. So before anyone could create a computing machine, the theory about how such a machine could work had to be figured out by mathematicians. It was the growth of this theory from hundreds of years ago that made possible the revolution in computer software that we see today. In a way, the present and future of computing and Machine Intelligence belong to great minds from our past.

In 1652, Blaise Pascal, while a 19-year-old teenager, created an arithmetic machine that could add, subtract, multiply, and divide.

In 1679, German mathematician Gottfried Wilhelm Leibniz created a system of binary code that laid the groundwork for modern computing.

In 1834, English inventor Charles Babbage conceived a mechanical device that could be programmed with punch cards. While it was never actually built, its logical structure, boolean logic, is what nearly every modern computer relies on to function.

In 1842, Ada Lovelace becomes the world's first computer programmer. At 27 years old, she designed an algorithm for solving mathematical problems using Babbage's punch-card technology.

In 1847, George Boole created an algebra capable of reducing all values to Boolean results. Boolean logic is what CPUs use to function and make decisions.

In 1936, Alan Turing discussed a theory describing how a machine could analyze and execute a series of instructions. His proof was published and is considered the bases of modern computer science.

In 1943, a neurophysiologist, Warren McCulloch, and a mathematician, Walter Pitts, co-wrote a paper theorizing how neurons in the human brain might function. Then they modeled their theory by building a simple neural network with electrical circuits.

In 1950, Alan Turing proposed the notion of a "learning machine." This machine could learn from the world like human beings do and eventually become artificially intelligent. He theorized about intelligence and described what was to become known as the "Turing Test" of machine intelligence. Intelligence, Turing mused, wasn't well defined but we humans seem to have it and to recognize it in others when we experience them using it. Thus, should we encounter a computer and can't tell it is a computer when we interact with it, then we could consider it intelligent too. What goes on under the hood doesn't matter, just like it doesn't matter how the brain of the person next to you does what it does, you know by interacting with that person that he or she is intelligent.

In 1951, Marvin Minsky, with the help of Dean Edmonds, created the first artificial neural network. It was called SNARC (Stochastic Neural Analog Reinforcement Calculator).

In 1952, Arthur Samuel begins working on some of

the first machine learning programs at IBM's Poughkeepsie Laboratory. Samuel was a pioneer in the fields of artificial intelligence and computer gaming. One of the first things they built was a machine that could play checkers. More importantly, this checkers-playing program could learn and improve its game.

In 1957, Frank Rosenblatt, while working at the Cornell Aeronautical Laboratory, creates the perceptron. It is an algorithm that through supervised learning is able to "learn" to use binary classifiers to decide if an input (vector of numbers) belongs to a particular class. The perceptron caused something of a storm in the media, leading some to suggest the navy (the project was funded by the US Office of Naval Research) would soon have a machine that could, as the New York Times put it at the time, "walk, talk, see, write, reproduce itself, and be conscious of its existence." Unfortunately, the hype was all... hype. The perceptron hit a wall when researches working with it discovered it could only be trained to learn a small number of classes of patterns. This caused the field to stagnate for many years.

In 1959, while working at IBM, Arthur Samuel coined the phrase "Machine Learning". Machine Learning was developed as part of the quest in the development of Artificial Intelligence. The goal of Machine Learning was to have machines learn from data. But despite its early start, Machine Learning was largely abandoned in the development of Artificial Intelligence. Like work on the perceptron, progress in Machine Learning lagged as Artificial Intelligence moved to the study of expert systems.

Eventually, this focus on a logical, knowledge-based approach to Artificial Intelligence caused a split between the disciplines. Machine Learning systems suffered from practical and theoretical problems in representation and acquiring large data sets to work with. Expert systems came to dominate by 1980, while statistical and probabilistic systems like Machine Learning fell out of favor. Early neural network research was also abandoned by Artificial Intelligence researchers and became its own field of study.

Machine Learning became its own discipline, mostly considered outside the purview of Artificial Intelligence, until the 1990s. Practically, all of the progress in Machine Learning from the 1960s through to the 1990s was theoretical, mostly statistics and probability theory. But while not much seemed to be accomplished, the theory and algorithms produced in these decades would prove to be the tools needed to re-energize the discipline. At this point, in the 1990s, the twin engines of vastly increased computer processing power and the availability of large datasets brought on a sort of renaissance for Machine Learning. Its goals shifted from the general notion of achieving artificial intelligence to a more focused goal of solving real-world problems, employing methods it would borrow from probability theory and statistics, ideas generated over the previous few decades. This shift and the subsequent successes it enjoyed, brought the field of Machine Learning back into the fold of Artificial Intelligence, where it resides today as a sub-discipline under the Artificial Intelligence umbrella.

However, Machine Learning was, continues to be, and might remain a form of Specific Artificial Intelligence. SAI are software algorithms able to learn a single or small range of items, which cannot be generalized to the world at large. The ultimate goal of artificial intelligence research is to develop a Generalized

Artificial Intelligence (GAI), which will not only be able to learn about the world but to generalize that knowledge and use it to learn about new things it has never encountered before. To this date, GAI remains an elusive goal, one many believe will never be reached. However, this does not take away from the fact that Machine Learning algorithms, even if they are specific artificial intelligence (SAI), are changing the world and will have an enormous effect on the future.

Chapter 2:

Theories of Machine Learning

The goal of Machine Learning stated simply is to create machines capable of learning about the world so they can accomplish whatever tasks we want them to do. Sound simple enough. This is something every human being accomplishes without any effort. From birth until adulthood, human beings learn about the world until they are able to master it. Why should this goal be so difficult for machines?

But even after 70 years of dedicated effort, the goal of general artificial intelligence remains elusive. As of today, there is nothing even approaching what could be called a Generalized Artificial Intelligence (GAI). That is an AI capable of learning from experience with the world, and from that learning becoming capable of acting in the world with intelligence. Like a child transitions from a relatively helpless being at birth, spends the next decade or two experiencing its world, language, culture, and physical reality surrounding it, then finally becomes an intelligent adult with an astounding general intelligence. A human being can learn to solve crossword puzzles in seconds, merely by a quick examination of the wording of the questions and the design of the field of squares. Drawing on a knowledge of language, puzzles, and the fact we often put letters in little boxes, a human being can infer how to do a crossword from previous, unrelated experiences. This simple task would absolutely baffle the most powerful artificial intelligence on Earth if it had not been specifically trained to do crossword puzzles.

Early Artificial Intelligence started out as an attempt to understand and employ the rules of thought. The assumption was that thinking is a chain of logical inference. Such a rules-based system might work like this:

Assertion: birds can fly
Fact: a robin is a bird
Inference: robins can fly

Therefore, early Artificial Researchers claimed, encoding thousands of such inferences in massive databases would allow a machine to make intelligent claims about the world. A machine equipped with such a database should be able to make inferences about the world and display an intelligence to rival human intelligence.

Unfortunately, researchers using this rules-based approach very quickly ran into problems. To continue with our bird example, what about flightless birds like the ostrich, or penguin, or emu? What about a bird with a broken wing that, at least temporarily, cannot fly? What do we call a bird in a small cage, where it cannot fly because of the bars? To human minds confronted with these exceptions, these questions are simple — of course, they are birds because flight, although available to most birds, does not define birdness.

Rules-based Artificial Intelligence researchers developed language to accommodate their rules of inference and these languages were flexible enough to accept and deal with such deviations as flightless birds. But writing down and programming all these distinctions, the deviations from the rule proved far more complicated than anticipated. Imagine attempting to code every exception to every rule of inference. The task quickly becomes Herculean and impossible for mere mortals.

The rise of probabilistic systems was in response to this choke point for these inference methods of artificial intelligence. Probabilistic systems are fed enormous amounts of relevant data about a subject like birds and are left to infer what they have in common (sometimes guided with classifying labels – supervised or semi-supervised, sometimes with no labels at all – unsupervised). These commonalities are used to modify the algorithm itself until its output approaches the desired output for the data in question.

This system works okay for birds or cats, but not so good for a more abstract idea like flight. Being fed images of thousands of things flying might allow an Artificial Intelligence to understand the concept of flight, but this learning tends to also label clouds as flying, or the sun, or a picture of an antenna on the top of a building with the sky as a backdrop. And the concept of flight is much more concrete than something truly abstract, like love or syntax.

So probabilistic Artificial Intelligence, what we are calling Machine Learning, switched from attempting to mimic or match human thought and to deal with concrete, real-world problems that it could solve. This transition in goals sparked the Machine Learning revolution. By focusing on concrete, real-world problems rather than generalized ideas, the algorithms of Machine Learning were able to achieve very powerful, very precise predictions of future states and to apply those predictions to new data.

Machine Learning today is considered a subset of Artificial Intelligence. The purpose of Machine Learning is to develop a software that can learn for itself. Essentially, researchers present a set of data with labels to a piece of software. The software ingests these examples and the relevant labels provided and attempt to extrapolate rules from the data and labels in order to make decisions on data it has never seen before. This rules-based system to make new matches is called a classifier.

The name for this approach to handling data is Computational Learning Theory. It is highly theoretical and mathematical, using statistics in particular. Computation Learning Theory is the study and analysis of machine learning algorithms. Learning Theory deals with inductive learning, a method known as supervised learning.

The goal of supervised learning is to correctly label new data as it is encountered, in the process reducing both the number of mislabels and the speed of the pattern matching process itself. However, there are hard limits to the performance of Machine Learning algorithms. These are the fact that data sets used for training are always finite and that the future is uncertain. These facts mean that the results of Machine Learning systems will be probabilistic — it is very difficult to guarantee a particular algorithm's accuracy. Instead of guarantees, then researchers will place upper and lower bounds on the probability of an algorithm's success at classification.

Chapter 3:

Approaches to Machine Learning

There is no formal definition of the approaches to Machine Learning, however, it is possible to separate the approaches into five loose groups. This chapter will identify these groups and describe their individual philosophical approaches to Machine Learning. Each of these philosophies has been successful in solving different categories of problems that humans need to deal with.

Finally, we will examine 3 real-world methods employed in actual Machine Learning, where some of these philosophies are turned into working systems. Where the rubber hits the road, so to speak.

Philosophies of Machine Learning

Artificial Intelligence has always been inspired by human cognition. And even though the philosophical methods described below rely heavily on complex math and statistics, each of them is an attempt to mimic, if not the process of human cognition, then at least the means whereby human cognition seems to function. This is an artificial intelligence that does not concern itself with how people or machines think, but only with whether the results of such thinking produce meaningful results.

Inverse Deduction

Human beings are hard-wired to fill in gaps. From the attachment of the ocular nerve to the retina (creating a black spot in our vision where we can't actually see) to creating faces where none exist (the face in the moon, for example), our brains are designed to fill in details in order to make patterns. This is a form of pattern induction. Deduction is the opposite. It is the process of moving from general experience to individual details. Inductive Artificial Intelligence is a more mathematical approach to this gap in the pattern filling. For example, if our algorithm knows 5 + 5 = 10, then it still is able to induce an answer if we give it 5 and ask it what needs to be added to this 5 to end up with 10. The system must answer the question "what knowledge is missing?" The required knowledge to answer this question is generated through the ingestion of data sets.

Making Connections

Another philosophy of Artificial Intelligence attempts to mimic some functions of the human brain. Scientists have been studying how human brains function for decades, and some researchers in Artificial Intelligence, beginning in earnest in the 1950s, have attempted to represent, mathematically, the neural architecture of the human brain. We call this approach neural network. They are composed of many mathematical nodes, analogous to neurons in the brain. Each node has an input, a weight, and an output. They are often layered, with the output of some neurons becoming the input of others. These systems are trained on data sets and with each iteration, the weights attributed to each node is adjusted as required in order to more closely approximate the desired output. The neural network approach has had much of the success in machine learning, lately in particular, because it is suited for dealing with large amounts of data. It is important to understand, however, that the term neural net is more of an inspiration than an attempt to replicate how human brains actually function. The complex interconnected web of neurons in the human brain is not something a neural net attempts to emulate. Instead, it is a series of mathematical, probabilistic inputs and outputs that attempts to model the results of the human neural activity.

Evolution

This approach is to mimic biological evolution. A variety of algorithms are tasked with solving a problem and exposed to an environment where they compete to produce the desired output. Each individual algorithm has a unique set of characteristics with which it can attempt to accomplish the task. After each iteration, the most successful algorithms are rewarded just like a successful animal in nature with higher fitness, meaning they are more likely to pass their features on to the next generation. Those that do continue to the next iteration can cross their feature sets with other successful algorithms, mimicking sexual reproduction. Add in some random "mutations" and you have the next generation, ready to iterate over the data again. This method can produce some powerful learning in its algorithms.

Bayesian

The Bayesian approach uses probabilistic inference to deal with uncertainty. It is a method of statistical inference where Bayes' theorem is employed to update hypothesis probabilities as new evidence becomes available. After a number of iterations, some hypotheses become more likely than others. A real-world example of this approach is Bayesian spam filtering. How it works is fairly simple. It has a collection of words that it compares to in the content of emails. It compares these words to the contents of email messages, increasing or decreasing the probability of the email being spam according to what it finds. Bayesian algorithms have been quite successful over the last two decades because they are adept at building structured models to real-world problems which have previously been considered intractable.

By Analogy

The fifth philosophical approach to Machine Learning involves using an analogy. This is yet another tactic borrowed from human cognition. Reasoning by analogy is a powerful tool humans use to incorporate new information by comparing it to similar information that is already known. By comparing this new information to established categories in our mental repertoire, human beings are able to classify and incorporate new information even when very little detail about this new information has been provided. The label for this approach is the "nearest neighbor" principle – basically asking what this new information is more similar too and categorizing it based on its similarity to known items. This approach is used in Support Vector Machines and until recently was likely the most powerful Machine Learning philosophy in use. An example of a real-world Support Vector Machine can be found in features like movie recommendations. If you and a stranger have given 5 stars to one movie and only one star to a different movie, the algorithm will recommend another movie that this stranger has rated favorably, assuming by analogy that your tastes are similar, and therefore, you will appreciate this movie recommendation as well.

What these philosophical approaches to Machine Learning tell us is twofold — the discipline, despite its roots in the mid-20th century, is still a nascent discipline that continues to grow into its own understanding. After all, Machine Learning is attempting to model the capacity of the most complex device in the known universe, the human brain.

At the same time, it is important to understand, as the history of artificial intelligence demonstrates, that we can see there is no "best" approach to Machine Learning. The "best" approach is only the best approach *for now*. Tomorrow, a new insight might surpass everything that's been accomplished to date, and pave a new path for artificial intelligence to follow.

At this point, we need to ask the question — how do collections of computer code and mathematics manage described thus far managed to learn? Here are the three most common methods currently in use to get computer algorithms to learn.

Supervised and Semi-supervised Learning Algorithms

In the supervised approach to Machine Learning, researchers first construct a mathematical model of a data set which includes the expected inputs and the required outputs. The data this produces is called training data and consists of sets of training examples (input and desired output). Each of these training examples is comprised of one or more inputs, along with the desired output – the supervisory signal. In semi-supervised learning, some of the desired output values are missing from the training examples.

Through iteration, that is, running the training data through the learning algorithm repeatedly, the learning algorithm develops a function to match the desired outputs from the inputs of the training data. During the iteration, this function is optimized by the learning algorithm. When this system is deemed ready, new data sets are introduced that are missing the desired outputs – these are known as the testing sets. At this point, errors or omission in the training data may become more obvious and the process can be repeated with new or more accurate output requirements. An algorithm that successfully modifies itself to improve the accuracy of its predictions or outputs can be said to have successfully learned to perform a task.

Supervised and semi-supervised learning algorithms include two classes of data handling — classification and regression. When outputs are limited by a constrained set of possible values, classification learning algorithms are employed. But when the outputs can be returned as a numerical value in a range of possible values, regression learning algorithms are the best fit.

Finally, there is similarity learning. While closely related to regression and classification learning, the goal of similarity learning is to examine data sets and determine how similar or different the information sets are. Similarity learning can be used in tasks such as ranking, recommendation systems (Netflix recommended anyone?), visual identity tracking, facial recognition/verification, and speaker (audio) verification.

Unsupervised Learning Algorithms

In unsupervised learning, algorithms are simply given large data sets containing only inputs. Their goal is to find structure in the data, grouped, or clustered data points that can be compared to new data sets. Unsupervised learning algorithms learn from data that has no labels and has not been organized or classified before being submitted. Instead of attempting to produce a required output prompted by supervisory systems, these algorithms attempt to find commonalities in the inputs they receive, which they then apply to new data sets. They react when these commonalities are found, missing, or broken in each new data set. Unsupervised learning algorithms are used in diverse fields including density estimation in statistics and the summarizing and explanation of data features. This type of learning can also be useful in fraud detection, where the goal is to find anomalies in input data.

Cluster analysis is when unsupervised learning algorithms break down a set of observations about data in clusters (subsets) so that the information within each cluster is similar based on one or more predefined criteria. Information drawn from other clusters will be internally similar, while dissimilar from each other. There are different approaches to data clustering, which are derived from making alternative assumptions about the structure of the data.

Reinforcement Learning

Reinforcement learning is an approach to Machine Learning that attempts to "reward" systems for taking actions in its environment that are in alignment with the objectives of the system. In this way, software trains itself using trial and error over sets of data until it induces the reward state. This field is actually quite large and not solely the purview of Machine Learning. It is also employed in disciplines like game theory, swarm intelligence, simulation-based optimization, information theory, and more.

Reinforcement learning for Machine Learning often employs an environment characterized by a Markov Decision Process – that is, a mathematical model to deal with a situation where the cause of the outcome is part random and part under control of the software decision maker. In addition, reinforcement learning algorithms typically employ dynamic programming techniques. This is a method whereby tasks are broken down into sub-tasks, where possible, to be regrouped once each sub-task has been accomplished into a solution for the main task. Reinforcement learning algorithms do not need to assume there is an exact model of the Markov Decision Process for them to employ. Instead, these algorithms are successfully employed when such exact models are not feasible.

Typical uses for Machine Learning reinforcement learning algorithms are in learning to play games against human opponents or in self-driving/autonomous vehicles.

Chapter 4:

Machine Learning and Artificial Intelligence

As with many complex ideas, classifying Machine Learning and Artificial Intelligence is often subject to debate, especially when the discussion becomes more specific and concrete. However, at a very general level, we can see Artificial Intelligence as an umbrella term that encompasses Machine Learning and several other attempts to design machines that can think.

Artificial Intelligence is the attempt to build machines that act like us. That is, machines that are "smart," that act with intelligence. There is very little debate in the scholarly world about what "intelligence" means because words like "smart" and "intelligent" are both politically loaded and intellectually fuzzy. Neither psychology nor neuroscience has effectively defined them with the precision required to apply to a machine driven by mathematics. In fact, even Alan

Turing's "Turing Test" was not meant be taken so literally. Turing was a very smart individual and the depth of the argument around his Turing Test is worth examining. What Turing was suggesting was, because human beings don't understand how human intelligence functions, let alone how machine intelligence might function, and also because not all human behavior can be considered intelligence, it would be best, should we come up against a computer program that could fool us into thinking it is human, to consider this machine intelligent. To put it simply, Turing was saying something like "smart is as smart does." Thus, the focus of Machine Learning researchers is not to understand intelligence, to classify it and define it as a goal to reach, but rather they use their skills to build software capable of learning and behaving in ways we might consider intelligent and let the philosophers debate the meaning of the word.

Thus, artificial intelligence is the idea of making machines that learn and act with intelligence. Machines that when we examine their behavior, leads us to believe they are smart. But this does not mean we consider a chess playing program intelligent at a human level. Sure, it can beat us at chess (or go, or the TV show Jeopardy, and so on), but ask any of these machines to answer a question they have not been previously trained to deal with and they become practically mindless. This stark difference between human intelligence and current machine intelligence is due to the general nature of human intelligence. Human beings can be intelligent in anything in a very short order. We can generalize our learning from one set of experiences and apply them to new and novel experiences in a way even the most powerful artificial intelligence programs today cannot hope to imitate. This is the ultimate goal of Machine Learning and artificial intelligence in general, what is known as general artificial intelligence. To date, there is no software that even approaches this kind of intelligence.

Nevertheless, advances in artificial intelligence are amazing and accelerating. This is due in part to the many different approaches employed to achieve the goal of artificial machine intelligence.

As we've seen above, Machine Learning is the use of data sets and algorithms to allow software to "learn," to identify relevant aspects of that data. That could be to identify similarities in this data or spot anomalies in it. While it is not human intelligence, it excels at this particular type of human intelligence to a degree exponentially better and faster than even the brightest human minds. If we keep in mind to what an astounding degree Machine Learning has outpaced human thinking in this very specific task, and imagine this specific task being combined in the future with other types of Machine Learning into a more generalized machine "mind", we can begin to get a sense of what might be awaiting us in the not too distant future, when this mind, a general artificial intelligence is born.

Chapter 5:

Machine Learning and Neural Networks

Neural networks were first developed in the late 1950s as a means to build learning systems that were modeled on our understanding of how the human brain functions. Despite their name, however, there is little resemblance between a neural network and a human brain. Mostly the name serves as a metaphor and as inspiration. Each "neuron" in a Neural Network is consists of a "node," a piece serial processing code designed to iterate over a problem until coming up with a solution at which point the result is passed on to the next neuron in the layer, or to the next layer if the current layer's processing is complete. In contrast, the human brain is capable of true parallel processing, by nature of the complex interconnections of its neurons and the fact its processing specialties are located in different areas of the brain (vision, hearing, smell, etc.), all of which can process signals simultaneously.

Neural networks are a sub-set of Machine Learning. They consist of software systems that mimic some aspects of human neurons. Neural Networks pass data through interconnected nodes. The data is analyzed, classified, and then passed on to the next node, where further classification and categorization may take place. The first layer of any Neural Network is the input layer, while the last is the output layer (these can be the same layer, as they were in the first, most primitive neural networks). Between is any number of hidden layers that do the work of dealing with the data presented by the input layer. Classical Neural Networks usually contain two to three layers. When a Neural Network is consists of more layers, it is referred to as Deep Learning. Such Deep Learning systems can have dozens or even hundreds of layers.

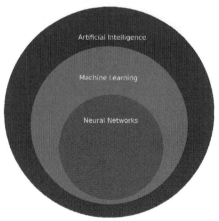

Feedforward Neural Networks

The first and most simple form of Neural Networks is called feedforward. As the name implies, data flows through a feedforward network in one direction, from the input, through the node layers containing the neurons and exits through the output layer. Unlike more modern neural networks, feedforward networks do not cycle or iterate over their data. They perform a single operation on the input data and they provide their solution in an output stream.

Single-layer perceptron
This is the simplest form of a feedforward neural network with one layer of nodes. The input is sent to each node already weighted and depending on how the node calculates the input and its weight, a minimal threshold may or not be met, and the neuron either fires (taking the "activated" value) or does not fire (taking the "deactivated" value).

Multi-layer perceptron
Multi-layer perceptrons, as the name suggests, are consist of two or more (sometimes many more) layers, with the output of the upper layer becoming the input

of the lower layer. Because there are many layers, this form of neural network often takes advantage of backpropagation, where the produced output is compared with the expected output, and the degree of error fed backward through the network to adjust the weights on the appropriate nodes, all with the intention of producing an output closer to the desired output state. Each error correction is tiny, so often a great number of iterations are required to achieve a "learned" state. At this point, the neural network is no longer considered a feedforward system proper. It is algorithms such as these multi-layer networks with backpropagation that have become some of the most successful and powerful Machine Learning devices in the field.

Recurrent Neural Networks

Recurrent Neural Networks propagate data in both directions, forward like feedforward networks but also backward from later to earlier processing stages. One of the main strengths of recurrent neural networks is the ability to remember previous states. Before recurrent neural networks, a neural network would forget previous tasks once it was asked to begin a new one. Imagine reading a comic but forgetting the content of the previous cells as you read the next one. Recurrent neural networks allow information to persist, meaning they can take input from subsequent events and "remember" their experience in previous ones. Put simply, recurrent neural networks are a series of input and output networks with the output of the first becoming the input of the second, the second's output the input of the third, and so on. This cycling allows Recurrent Neural Networks to develop closer and closer approximations to the desired output.

Backpropagation

Theoretical development of backpropagation came from Paul Werbos' Ph.D. thesis in 1974. Unfortunately, due to complications and difficulties encountered by those attempts to create Neural Networks (both theoretical and hardware-related), Neural Networks did not really catch on until the 1980s, when processor power and large numerous data sets became available for training and testing.

The application of backpropagation is highly mathematical but can be summarized like this: each iteration of a neural network produces a mathematical degree of error between the desired output and the actual output of the network. Each neuron in a neural network has a weight attached to it for the purposes of modifying its calculation on the input it receives. Backpropagation uses mathematics (probability statistics) when it is possible, to calculate the derivative of the error between expected and actual outputs. This derivative is then used on the next iteration to adjust the weight applied to each of the neurons. Each subsequent iteration produces a smaller error. Imagine a basketball dropped somewhere in a skateboard half-pipe. It will roll down towards the center and up the other side, then reverse direction and roll towards the center again. Each time, it will roll less distance up the side before reversing direction. Eventually, gravity will bring the ball to a stable state in the center. In the same way, backpropagation reduces the error produced in each iteration as it brings the actual output closer to the desired output.

We have seen above that the goal of Machine Learning is to make software able to learn from the data it experiences. This is the goal of Neural Networks as well, but while Machine Learning makes decisions based on what data it has seen before, Neural Networks are designed to learn and make intelligent decisions on their own. This is particularly useful when the patterns being searched for are too numerous or complex for a software programmer to extract and submit as part of an input training data set.

Chapter 6:

Machine Learning and Big Data

Big Data is pretty much what it sounds like — the practice of dealing with large volumes of data. And by large, we are talking about astoundingly huge amounts of data — gigabytes, terabytes, petabytes of data. A petabyte, to put this size into perspective, is 10 to the 15th bytes. Written out that is 1 PB = 1,000,000,000,000,000 bytes. When you consider that a single byte is equivalent in storage to a single letter like an 'a' or 'x', the scale of the data sets being dealt with my Big Data is truly awe-inspiring. And these sizes are increasing every day.

The term Big Data comes from the 1990s, although computer scientists have been dealing with large volumes of data for decades. What sets Big Data apart from data sets before is the fact the size of data sets began to overwhelm the ability of traditional data analytics software to deal with it. New database storage systems had to be created (Hadoop for example) just to hold the data and new software written to be able to deal with so much information in a meaningful way.

Today the term Big Data brings with it a series of assumptions and practices that have made it a field all its own. Most Big Data discussions begin with the 3 V's. Big data is data containing more variety arriving in increasing volumes and with increasing velocity (acceleration would be an accurate term to use here, but then we'd lose the alliteration).

Volume

The term volume refers to the vast amount of data available. When the term Big Data was coined in the early 2000s, the amount of data available for analysis was overwhelming. Since then, the volume of data created has grown exponentially. In fact, the volume of data produced has become so vast then new storage solutions had to be created just to deal with it. This increase in available data shows no sign of slowing and is, in fact, increasing geometrically by doubling every two years.

Velocity

Along with the rise in the amount of data being created is the speed at which it is produced. Things like smartphones, RFID chips, and real-time facial recognition produce not only enormous amounts of data, this data is produced in real time and must be dealt with as it is created. If not processed in real time, it must be stored for later processing. The increasing speed of this data arriving strains the capacity of bandwidth, processing power, and storage space to contain it for later use.

Variety

Data does not get produced in a single format. It is stored numerically in detailed databases, produced in structure-less text and email documents, and stored digitally in streaming audio and video. There is stock market data, financial transactions, and so on, all of it uniquely structured. So not only must large amounts of data be handled very quickly, it is produced in many formats that require distinct methods of handling for each type.

Lately, two more V's have been added:

Value

Data is intrinsically valuable, but only if you are able to extract this value from it. Also, the state of input data, whether it is nicely structured in a numeric database or unstructured text message chains, affects its value. The less structure a data set has, the more work needs to be put into it before it can be processed. In this sense, well-structured data is more valuable than less-structured data.

Veracity

Not all captured data is of equal quality. When dealing with assumptions and predictions parsed out of large data sets, knowing the veracity of the data being used has an important effect on the weight given to the information studying it generates. There are many causes that limit data veracity. Data can be biased by the assumptions made by those who collected it. Software bugs can introduce errors and omission in a data set. Abnormalities can reduce data veracity like when two wind speed sensors next to each other report different wind directions. One of the sensors could be failing, but there is no way to determine this from data itself. Sources can also be of questionable veracity — in a company's social media feed are a series of very negative reviews. Were they human or bot created? Human error, as in a person signing up to a web service enters in their phone number incorrectly. And there are many more ways data veracity can be compromised.

The point of dealing with all this data is to identify useful detail out of all the noise — businesses can find ways to reduce costs, increase speed and efficiency, design new products and brands, and make more intelligent decisions. Governments can find similar benefits in studying the data produced by their citizens and industries.

Here are some examples of current uses of Big Data.

Product Development
Big Data can be used to predict customer demand. Using current and past products and services to classify key attributes, they can then model these attributes' relationships and their success in the market.

Predictive Maintenance
Buried in structured data are indices that can predict mechanical failure of machine parts and systems.

Year of manufacture, make and model, and so on, provide a way to predict future breakdowns. Also, there is a wealth of unstructured data in error messages, service logs, operating temperature, and sensor data. This data, when correctly analyzed, can predict problems before they happen so maintenance can be deployed preemptively, reducing both cost and system downtime.

Customer Experience

Many businesses are nothing without their customers. Yet acquiring and keeping customers in a competitive landscape is difficult and expensive. Anything that can give a business an edge will be eagerly utilized. Using Big Data, businesses can get a much clearer view of the customer experience by examining social media, website visit metrics, call logs, and any other recorded customer interaction to modify and improve the customer experience. All in the interests of maximizing the value delivered in order to acquire and maintain customers. Offers to individual customers can become not only more personalized but more relevant and accurate. By using Big Data to identify problematic issues, businesses can handle them quickly and effectively, reducing customer churn and negative press.

Fraud & Compliance

While there may be single rogue bad actors out there in the digital universe attempting to crack system security, the real threats are from organized, well-financed teams of experts, sometimes teams supported by foreign governments. At the same time, security practices and standards never stand still but are constantly changing with new technologies and new approaches to hacking existing ones. Big Data helps identify data patterns suggesting fraud or tampering and aggregation of these large data sets makes regulatory reporting much faster.

Operation Efficiency

Not the sexiest topic, but this is the area in which Big Data is currently providing the most value and return. Analyze and assess production systems, examine customer feedback and product returns, and examine a myriad of other business factors to reduce outages and waste, and even anticipate future demand and trends. Big Data is even useful in assessing current decision-making processes and how well they function in meeting demand.

Innovation

Big Data is all about relations between meaningful labels. For a large business, this can mean examining how people, institutions, other entities, and business processes intersect, and use any interdependencies to drive new ways to take advantage of these insights. New trends can be predicted and existing trends can be better understood. This all leads to understanding what customers actually want and anticipate what they may want in the future. Knowing enough about individual customers may lead to the ability to take advantage of dynamic pricing models. Innovation driven by Big Data is really only limited by the ingenuity and creativity of the people curating it.

Machine Learning is also meant to deal with large amounts of data very quickly. But while Big Data is focused on using existing data to find trends, outliers, and anomalies, Machine Learning uses this same data to "learn" these patterns in order to deal with future data proactively. While Big Data looks to the past and present data, Machine Learning examines the present data to learn how to deal with the data that will be collected in the future. In Big Data, it is people who define what to look for and how to organize and structure this information. In Machine Learning, the algorithm teaches itself what is important through iteration over test data, and when this process is completed, the algorithm can then go ahead to new data it has never experienced before.

Chapter 7:

Machine Learning and Regression

Machine Learning can produce two distinct output types — classification and regression. A classification problem involves an input that requires an output in the form of a label or category. Regression problems, on the other hand, involve an input that requires an output value as a quantity. Let's look at each form in more detail.

Classification Problems

Classification problems are expected to produce an output that is a label or category. That is to say, a function is created from an examination of the input data that produces a discrete output. A familiar example of a classification problem is whether a given email is spam or not spam.

Classification can involve probability, providing a

probability estimate along with its classification. 0.7 spam, for example, suggests a 70% chance an existing email is a spam. If this percentage meets or exceeds the acceptable level for a spam label, then the email is classified as spam (we have spam folders in our email programs, not 65% spam folders), otherwise, it is classified as not spam. One common method to determine classification problem's algorithm probability of accuracy is to compare the results of its predictive model against the actual classification of the data set it has examined. On a data set of 5 emails, for example, where the algorithm has successfully classified 4 out of 5 of the emails in the set, the algorithm could be said to have an accuracy of 80%. Of course, in a real-world example, the training data set would be much more massive.

Regression problems

In a regression problem, the expected output is in the form of an unlimited numerical range. The price of a used car is a good example. The input might be the year, color, mileage, condition, etc., and the expected output in a dollar value, i.e.: $4,500 - $6,500. The skill (error) of a regression algorithm can be determined using various mathematical techniques. A common skill measure for regression algorithms is to calculate the root mean squared error, RMSE.

Although it is possible to modify each of the above methods to produce each other's result (that is, turn a classification algorithm into a regression algorithm and vice versa), the output requirements of the two define each algorithm quite clearly:

1. Classification algorithms produce a discrete category result which can be evaluated for accuracy, while regression algorithms cannot.
2. Regression algorithms produce a range result and can be evaluated using root mean squared error, while classification algorithms cannot.

So, while Machine Learning employs both types of methods for problem-solving (classification and regression), what method is employed for any particular problem depends on the nature of the problem and how the solution needs to be presented.

Chapter 8:

Machine Learning and the Cloud

Cloud computing has entered the public consciousness. As a metaphor, it is powerful because it takes a complex activity and turns it into a simple idea. But cloud computing is a complex and expensive undertaking. It involves the integration of hundreds, thousands, or even tens of thousands of computer servers in a massive data center (a single Amazon data center can host as many as 80,000 servers). This "raw iron" serves as the backbone of the cloud service. The servers operate virtual machine managers called hypervisors, which can be either software or hardware that uses the raw processing power of the existing data center servers to simulate other software, be that individual programs or entire operating systems.

The advantage of cloud computing is the fact the cost associated with all that hardware in the data center is absorbed by the company providing the cloud services. This includes the building and infrastructure to operate the hardware, the electricity to power it, and the staff to maintain, service, update, and repair hardware and software systems.

These companies monetize their hardware and virtualized software by selling it on demand to whoever wants to use it, be that other companies, governments, universities, or individuals. And even though the cloud service is more expensive than purchasing and using servers of their own, the advantage is in the on-demand nature of the service. A company may have a spike in its retail website use around Christmas, for example, where demand surges and would overwhelm the servers that are able to operate without issue on the rest of the year. Instead of having to purchase more hardware to manage this spike in use, hardware that would remain essentially dormant the rest of the year (though still consuming electricity, requiring maintenance, and updates by trained staff, and so on), this company could instead acquire a cloud services account and "virtualize" part of its website business using load balancing to make sure its servers are not overwhelmed. If demand is even more than expected, in a matter of moments, more servers can be spun up to carry the demand. As traffic decreases late at night, or for whatever reason, these extra virtual servers can be shut down, no longer costing the company money to operate.

Previously, we've discussed the forces that allowed Machine Learning to come into its own, the historical development of the mathematical algorithms being used, the rise of very large, numerous sets of data, and the increasing power of computer processors. But even as these factors merged to make Machine Learning viable, it is extremely expensive. There are enormous resources required, from qualified software developers who know the math behind Machine Learning algorithms, to gaining access to large data sets either through business operations or purchase, to being able to afford the massive processing power to crunch all that data and allow an algorithm to learn. Access to Machine Learning has for the most part been only for governments, research organizations like universities, and large businesses.

The Cloud promises to change this. As Machine Learning systems are developed and refined by researchers and business ahead of the curve in the industry, they can often end up available to consumers in cloud-based services provided by companies like Amazon AWS, Google Cloud, and Microsoft Azure. Because these services can provide these algorithms on demand, the cost per use for them can be quite low. At the same time, cloud-based storage has become very reasonably priced, meaning those massive data sets needed for training and testing Machine Learning algorithms can be stored in the cloud as well, reducing cost for storage, the infrastructure required to carry the bandwidth needed to move such massive amounts of data, and the time required to make such transfers. The software and data can reside in the same cloud account, providing instant access, and no bandwidth costs.

Companies using cloud computing to implement Machine Learning do not need an IT department capable of creating and managing the AI infrastructure, as this is taken care of by the companies offering the cloud services.

Just as cloud-based services offer SaaS (software as a service) solutions, Machine Learning cloud services offer SDKs (software developer kits) and APIs (application programming interfaces) to embed Machine Learning functions into applications. These connections offer support for most programming languages, meaning developers working for the companies using the cloud-based solutions do not need to learn any new languages to harness the Machine Learning infrastructure. Developers can harness the power of Machine Learning processes directly in their applications, which is where the most value lies because most real-world use of Machine Learning systems today are transaction and operations-focused. Real-time loan applications, fraudulent transactions, mapping and route planning, facial recognition, voice authorization, and so on.

Benefits of Cloud-Based Machine Learning

It is possible to use one of the free open source Machine Learning frameworks such as CNTK, TensorFlow, and MXNet to create your own AI solutions, but even though the frameworks are free, the barriers to do it yourself approach can be prohibitive. We've touched on them above — overall cost for hardware and hardware maintenance, the cost for software maintenance, and the cost of acquiring and maintaining a team of AI specialists capable of designing and maintaining Machine Learning systems.

Cloud-based Machine Learning projects make it easy for a company or organization to use limited levels of resources during experimentation and training while providing a seamless ability to scale up for production and in the future as demand increases. Whereas in with an in-house Machine Learning option, after training has taken place and the algorithm is ready for production deployment, an entire infrastructure must be created around the software for outside systems to use it. With a cloud solution, production is often as simple as a few mouse clicks away.

Amazon AWS, Google Cloud Platform, and Microsoft Azure have many Machine Learning services that do not require knowledge of Artificial Intelligence, theories of Machine Learning, or even a data science team.

At this point, the big cloud service providers provide two basic kinds of Machine Learning offerings — general and specific. A specific offering, for example, is Amazon's Rekognition, an image-recognition Machine Learning implementation that can be run with a single command. On the other hand, if what you require is not available from one of these specific user options, all three services offer more generalized Machine Intelligence solutions requiring the user to create custom code and to be run on general-purpose services.

There has been an attempt to make services that offer more general-purpose Machine Learning services that are simpler to use, but as with many attempts at generalized software frameworks, the market hasn't embraced the concept because while being easier to use, the simplicity of the interface means it is not possible to get the custom requirements customers are looking for.

Chapter 9:

Machine Learning and the Internet of Things (IoT)

Perhaps the first Internet of Things was at Carnegie Mellon University in 1982 when a Coke machine was connected to the internet so it could report on its current stock levels, as well as the temperature of newly-loaded drinks.

But at that time, computer miniaturization had not progressed to the point it has today, so it was difficult for people at that time to conceive of very small devices connecting to the internet. As well, consumer wireless internet would not be available for another 15 years, meaning any internet connected device had to be fairly large and wired to its connection.

Today, the Internet of Things (IoT) refers to all the internet-connected devices in the world. Some are obvious like your smartphone, and some are not so obvious like a smart thermostat in your house. The term also applies to internet-connected devices that are part of a device like a sensor on an industrial robot's arm or the jet engine from a commercial jetliner.

A relatively simple explanation, but it is hard to conceive just how many IoT devices are around us, never mind how many will be in the near future. The following is a breakdown of some of the current Internet of Things devices currently in use, which is often broken down into the following categories:

Consumer Applications

The number of Internet of Things devices created for consumer use is expanding rapidly. From smartphones to connected vehicles to wearable health technology and health monitoring devices, the Internet of Things is entering our lives at a rapid pace.

Smart Home

Home automation is the concept of having your house manage its resources for you. Lighting, the resources in the fridge, air conditioning, security, media, and so on. The Internet of Things is critical to this philosophy because the means to manage and automate home resources comes through the ability of the, until now, separate devices being able to connect to the internet and possibly to each other. These connections allow the owner to adjust the lighting or temperature or view areas of the home when outside the home. At the same time, these devices are able to alert the owner, sending a warning that an external perimeter has been breached and offering a real-time video display of the culprit – more likely a raccoon than a burglar, but in either case, the devices can provide a feeling of control. Another example might be when your smart fridge notices your milk is 90% empty and automatically adds it to your electronic shopping list.

Clearly, the examples above and we could come up with many more currently being used, as well as all those not yet created that will be coming in the future, employ various kinds of Machine Learning. The security system above needs to determine something is moving in the backyard. Perhaps more advanced Machine Learning would even be able to distinguish a person from a small animal and not bother you at all. At the same time, it could possibly use facial recognition to determine it is only your neighbor come around to fetch a frisbee accidentally thrown over the adjoining fence.

The smart fridge not only needs to be able to classify the items it is holding, but to judge when enough of an item has been consumed to justify ordering more – clearly a Machine Learning problem since 70% consumed might mean less than a day left for a family of three, but 2 days' supply for a single person. These details will be learned, as a Machine Learning algorithm in your fridge first observes the occupants using the fridge and determines the correct quantities for reorder. When another person moves back in for the summer after college, a Machine Learning algorithm can observe and adjust its estimates accordingly. Over time, these predictive models can aggregate their data, allowing new instances of the algorithm to auto-correct for added or removed residents, based on the data sets of previous move ins and move outs.

Elder/Disabled Care

One of the Smart Home's strongest selling features is its ability to help care for people with disabilities. Among assistive technologies available is voice control to activate/deactivate or set features around the house — lighting, temperature, etc., and the ability to monitor for medical emergencies like seizures or falls. No doubt these features will expand, including an option for diagnosis and treatment suggestions, as well as the ability to interface with emergency services and local hospitals to notify and assist in dealing with medical emergencies.

Machine Learning in the home is already available in

terms of voice recognition and fall monitoring. It will be instrumental in more extensive medical monitoring, including the ability to "read" emotions and monitor our health via external and even internal sensors.

Here again, we see how the integration of the IoT and the health care system can provide a benefit, but behind many of these qualities of life improving devices is the predictive and anomaly detection capacity of Machine Learning algorithms.

Commercial Applications

Healthcare

We are entering the world of "Smart Healthcare," where computers, the internet, and artificial intelligence are merging to improve our quality of life. The Internet of Medical (or Health) Things (IoHT) is a specific application of the Internet of Things designed for health and medical related purposes. It is leading to the digitization of the healthcare system, providing connectivity between properly equipped healthcare services and medical resources.

Some Internet of (Heath) Things applications is to enable remote health monitoring and to operate emergency notification systems. This can range from blood pressure monitoring and glucose levels to the monitoring of medical implants in the body. In some hospitals, you will find "smart beds" that can detect patients trying to get up and adjust themselves to maintain healthy and appropriate pressure and support for the patient, without requiring the intervention of a nurse or other health professional. One report estimated these sorts of devices and technology could save the US health care system $300 billion in a year in increased revenue and decreased costs. The interactivity of medical systems has also led to the creation of "m-health," which is used to collect and analyze information provided by different connected resources like sensors and biomedical information collection systems.

Rooms can be equipped with sensors and other devices to monitor the health of senior citizens or the critically ill, ensuring their well-being, as well as monitor that treatments and therapies are carried out to provide comfort, regain lost mobility, and so on. These sensing devices are interconnected and can collect, analyze, and transfer important and sensitive information. In-home monitoring systems can interface with a hospital or other health-care monitoring stations.

There have been many advances in plastics and fabrics allowing for the creation of very low-cost, throw away "wearable" electronic IoT sensors. These sensors, combined with RFID technology are fabricated into paper or e-textiles, providing wirelessly-powered, disposable sensors.

Combined with Machine Learning, the health care IoHT ecosphere around each one of us can improve quality of life, guard against drug errors, encourage health and wellness, and respond to and even predict responses by emergency personnel. As a collection of technology and software, this future "smart" health care will cause a profound shift in medical care, where we no longer wait for obvious signs of illness to diagnose, but instead use the predictive power of Machine Learning to detect anomalies and predict future health issues long before human beings even know something might be wrong.

Transportation

The IoT assists various transportation systems in the integration of control, communications, and information processing. It can be applied throughout the entire transportation system — drivers, users, vehicles, and infrastructure. This integration allows for inter and even intra-vehicle communication, logistics and fleet management vehicle control, smart traffic control, electronic toll collection systems, smart parking, and even safety and road assistance.

Take logistics and fleet management, an IoT platform

provides continuous monitoring of cargo and asset locations and conditions using wireless sensors and send alerts when anomalies occur (damage, theft, delays, and so on). GPS, temperature, and humidity sensors can return data to the IoT platform where it can be analyzed and set on to the appropriate users. Users are then able to track in real-time the location and condition of vehicles and cargo and are then able to make the appropriate decisions based on accurate information. IoT can even reduce traffic accidents by providing drowsiness alerts and health monitoring for drivers to ensure they do not drive when they need rest.

As the IoT is integrated more and more with vehicles and the infrastructure required to move these vehicles around, the ability for cities to control and alleviate traffic congestion, for businesses to control and respond to issues with transportation of their goods, and for both of these groups to work together, increases dramatically. In an unforeseen traffic congestion due to an accident, for example, sensitive products (a patient in an ambulance on the way to Emergency, or produce or other time-sensitive items) could be put in the front of the queue to ensure they are delayed as little as possible, all without the need for traffic direction by human beings.

The potential rewards of such an integrated system are many, perhaps only limited by our imagination. Using IoT enabled statistics from traffic will allow for optimum traffic routing, which in term will reduce travel time and CO_2 emissions. Smart stop lights and road signs with variable-speed and information displays will communicate more and more with the onboard systems of vehicles, providing routing information to reduce travel time. And all of this technology is made possible by dedicated Machine Learning algorithms with access to the near endless flow of data from thousands and thousands of individual IoT sensors.

Building/Home Automation
As discussed above, IoT devices can be used in any kind of building, where they can monitor and control the electrical, mechanical, and electronic systems of these buildings. The advantages identified are:

- By integrating the internet with a building's energy management systems, it is possible to

create "smart buildings" where energy efficiency is driven by IoT.
- Real-time monitoring of buildings provides a means for reducing energy consumption and the monitoring of occupant behavior.
- IoT devices integrated into buildings provide information on how smart devices can help us understand how to use this connectivity in future applications or building designs.

When you read "smart" or "real-time" above, you should be thinking Machine Learning because it is these algorithms that can tie all of the sensor input together into something predictive and intelligent.

Industrial Applications

Manufacturing

Manufacturing equipment can be fitted with IoT devices for sensing, identification, communication, actuation monitoring, processing, and networking, providing a seamless integration between the manufacturing and control systems. This integration has permitted the creation of brand-new business and marketing options in manufacturing. This network control and management of manufacturing process control, asset and situation management, and manufacturing equipment set the IoT in the industrial application and smart manufacturing space, allowing features such as:

- Rapid manufacturing of new products.
- Real-time product and supply chain optimization by networking machine sensors and their control systems together.
- Allowing dynamic responses to product or market demand

The above is achieved by networking manufacturing machinery, control systems, and sensors together.

The IoT can be applied to employ digital control systems for automating process controls, manage service information systems in the optimization of plant safety and security, and maintain and control operator tools.

Machine Learning, when integrated into these networked systems, allows asset management and surveillance to maximize reliability by employing predictive maintenance and statistical evaluation. Real-time energy optimization is possible through the integration of the various sensor systems.

Machine Learning allows IoT to maximize reliability through asset management using predictive maintenance, statistical evaluation, and measurements.

The manufacturing industry has its own version of the Internet of Things, the industrial Internet of Things (IIoT). The estimated effect IIoT could have on the manufacturing sector is truly astounding. Growth due to the integration of the Internet of Things with manufacturing is estimated at a $12 trillion dollar increase in global GDP by 2030.

Data acquisition and device connectivity are imperative for IIoT. This is not the goal, but rather a necessary condition for developing something much greater. At the core of this will be interfacing Machine Learning algorithms with local IIoT devices. This has already been done in some instances with predictive maintenance, and this success will hopefully pave the way for new and much more powerful ways to allow these intelligent maintenance systems to reduce unforeseen downtime and provide increased productivity. How this will be realized is yet to be determined, but it will involve analysis of the Big Data provided by the manufacturing systems and IIoT devices, and lead to what is being called "cyber-physical systems". This term refers to the interface between human beings and the cyber world, and this system will eventually allow data collected from it into actionable information, decreasing costs, increasing safety, and boosting efficiency. As with so many implementations of Machine Learning in our world, it would seem the only limit to the advantages it can provide in the manufacturing sector relies on the limits of our imagination to take advantage of it.

A real-world example of this integrated approach was conducted by the University of Cincinnati in 2014. Industrial band-saws have belts that degrade and eventually, if not caught by routine inspection, break, presenting a hazard to the operators. In this experiment, a feedback system was created in which Industrial Internet of Things sensors monitored the status of the belt and returned this data to a predictive system, which could alert users when the band was likely to fail and when the best time to replace it would be. This system showed it was possible to save on costs, increase operator safety, and improve the user experience by integrating IIoT devices with Machine Learning algorithms.

Agriculture
The IoT allows farmers to collect data on all sorts of parameters, things like temperature, humidity, wind speed/direction, temperature, soil composition, and even pest infestations.

The collection of this data when combined with Machine Learning algorithms, allows farmers to automate some farm techniques such as making informed decisions to improve crop quality and quantity, minimize risk, reduce required crop management efforts, and minimize waste. Farmers can monitor soil temperature and moisture and use this data to decide on an optimum time to water or fertilize fields. In the future, Machine Learning can use historical and current weather data in combination with data returned from the Internet of Things devices embedded in the farm to further maximize these decision-making processes.

An example of a real-world combination of Machine Learning and IoT in agriculture took place in 2018, when Toyota Tsusho (member of the Toyota group which is parent to, among many other things, Toyota Motors) partnered with Microsoft and created fish farming tools employing the Microsoft Azure Internet of Things application suite for water management. The water pump in this facility uses Machine Learning systems provided by Azure to count fish on a conveyor belt and use this result to determine how effective the water flow was in the system. This one system employed both the Microsoft Azure IoT Hub and Microsoft Azure Machine Learning platforms.

Infrastructure Applications

The Internet of Things can be used for control and monitoring of both urban and rural infrastructure, things like bridges, railways, and off and on-shore wind farms. The IoT infrastructure can be employed to monitor changes and events in structural conditions that might threaten safety or increase risks to users.

The construction industry can employ the Internet of Things and receive benefits like an increase in productivity, cost savings, paperless workflows, time reduction, and better-quality work days for employees, while real-time monitoring and data analytics can save money and time by allowing faster decision-making processes. Coupling the Internet of Things with Machine Learning predictive solutions allows for a more efficient scheduling for maintenance and repair, as well as allowing for better coordination of tasks between users and service providers. Internet of Things deployments can even control critical infrastructure by allowing bridge access control to approaching ships, saving time and money. Large-scale deployment of IoT devices for the monitoring and operation of infrastructure will probably improve the quality of service, increase uptime, reduce the costs of operations, and increase incident management and emergency response coordination. Even waste-management could benefit from IoT deployments, allowing for the benefits of optimization and automation.

City Scale Uses

The Internet of Things has no upper limit to what it can encompass. Today, buildings and vehicles are routine targets for Internet of Things integration, but tomorrow, it will be cities that are the wide-scale target of this digital revolution. In many cities around the world, this integration is beginning with important effects on utilities, transportation, and even law enforcement. In South Korea, for example, an entire city is being constructed as the first of its kind, a fully equipped and wired city. Much of the city will be automated, requiring very little or even no human intervention. Songdo is nearly finished construction.

The city of Santander in Spain is taking a different approach. It does not have the benefit of being built from scratch, so instead, it has produced an app that is connected with over 10,000 sensors around the city. Things like parking search, a digital city agenda, environmental monitoring, and more have been integrated by the Internet of Things. Residents of the city download an app to their smartphones in order to access this network.

In San Jose California, an Internet of Things deployment has been created with several purposes — reducing noise pollution, improving air and water quality, and increasing transportation efficiency. In 2014, the San Francisco Bay Area partnered with Sigfox, a French company to deploy an ultra-narrow band wireless data network, the first such business-backed installation in the United States. They planned to roll out over 4000 more base stations to provide coverage to more than 30 U.S. cities.

In New York, all the vessels belonging to the city were connected, allowing 24/7 monitoring. With this wireless network, NYWW can control its fleet and passengers in a way that was simply not possible to imagine even a decade ago. Possible new applications for the network might include energy and fleet management, public Wi-Fi, security, paperless tickets, digital signage, among others.

Most of the developments listed above will rely on Machine Learning as the intelligent back-end to the forward-facing Internet of Things used to monitor and update all the components of any smart city. It would seem the next step, after the creation of smart cities through the integration of Internet of Things sensors and monitors with Machine Learning algorithms, would be larger, regional version. There does not seem to be any reason to suggest an upper limit. So "smart countries" may certainly be a possibility in the future.

Energy Management
So many electrical-using devices in our environment already boast an internet connection. In the future, these connections will allow communication with the utility from which they draw their power. The utility, in turn, will be able to use this information to balance energy generation with load usage and to optimize energy consumption over the grid. The Internet of Things will allow users to remotely control (and schedule) lighting, HVAC, ovens, and so on. On the utility's side, aspects of the electrical grid,

transformers, for example, will be equipped with sensors and communications tools, which the utility will use to manage and the distribution of energy.

Once again, the power of Machine Learning will provide the predictive models necessary to anticipate and balance loads, aided by the constant flow of information from Internet of Things devices located throughout the power grid. At the same time, these IoT monitors will also provide services levels and other information, so artificial intelligence systems can track and identify when components are reaching the end of life and need repair or replacement. No more surprise power outages, as components getting close to failure will be identified and repaired before they can threaten the power grid.

Environmental Monitoring

The Internet of Things can be used for environmental monitoring and usually, that application means environmental protection. Sensors can monitor air and water quality, soil and atmospheric conditions, and can even be deployed to monitor the movement of wildlife through their habitats. This use of the Internet of Things over large geographic areas means it can be used by tsunami or earthquake early-warning systems, which can aid emergency response services in providing more localized and effective aid. These IoT devices can include a mobile component. A standardized environmental Internet of Things will likely revolutionize environmental monitoring and protection.

Here, we can begin to see the geographic scalability of Machine Learning as it interfaces with the Internet of Things. While the city is impressive due to the number of sensors and devices it may have deployed throughout it, in a rural or natural environmental setting, the Internet of Things density of devices drops sharply, yet these huge geographical areas can come under the scrutiny of Machine Learning algorithms in ways still yet to be conceived.

Trends in IoT

The trend for the Internet of Things is clear — explosive growth. There were an estimated 8.4 billion IoT devices in 2017, a 31% increase from the year before. By 2020, worldwide estimates are 30 billion devices. At this point, the market value of these devices will be over $7 trillion. The amount of data these devices will produce is staggering. And when all this data is collected and ingested by Machine Learning algorithms, control and understanding of so many aspects of our lives, our cities, even our wildlife will increase dramatically.

Intelligence
Ambient Intelligence is an emerging discipline in which our environment becomes sensitive to us. It was not meant to be part of the Internet of Things but the trend seems to be that Ambient Intelligence and autonomous control are two disciplines into which the Internet of Things will make great inroads. Already research in these disciplines is shifting to incorporate the power and ubiquity of the IoT.

Unlike today, the future Internet of Things might be comprised of a good number of non-deterministic devices, accessing an open network where they can auto-organize. That is to say, a particular IoT device may have a purpose, but when required by other Internet of Things devices can become part of a group or swarm to accomplish a collective task that overrides its individual task in priority. Because these devices will be more generalized with a suite of sensors and abilities, these collectives will be able to organize themselves using the particular skills of each individual to accomplish a task, before releasing its members when the task is complete so they can continue on with their original purpose. These autonomous groups can form and disperse depending on the priority given to the task, and considering the circumstances, context and environment in which the situation is taking place.

Such collective action will require coordination and intelligence, which of course will need to be provided, at least in part, by powerful Machine Learning algorithms tasked with achieving these large-scale objectives. Even if the Internet of Things devices that are conscripted to achieve a larger goal have their own levels of intelligence, it will be assisted by artificial intelligence systems able to collate all the incoming data from the IoT devices responding to the goal and finding the best approach to solve any problems. Although swarm intelligence technology will also likely play a roll (see later in the book in the chapter on The Swarm), swarms cannot provide the predictive ability that crunching massive data sets by Machine Learning backed by powerful servers have.

Architecture

The system architecture of IoT devices is typically broken down into three main tiers. Tier one includes devices, Tier two is the Edge Gateway, and Tier three is the Cloud.

Devices are simply network-connected things with sensors and transmitters using a communication protocol (open or proprietary) to connect with an Edge Gateway.

The Edge Gateway is the point where incoming sensor data is aggregated and processed through systems to provide functionality including data pre-processing, securing cloud connections, and running WebSockets or even edge analytics.

Finally, Tier three includes the applications based in the cloud built for the Internet of Things devices. This tier includes database storage systems to archived sensor data. The cloud system handles communication taking place in all tiers and provides features like event queuing.

As data is passed from the Internet of Things, a new architecture emerges, the web of things, the application layer which processes the disparate sensor data from the Internet of Things devices into web applications, driving innovation in use-cases.

It is no great leap to assume this architecture does, and will even more in the future, require massive scalability in the network. One solution being deployed is fog (or edge) computing, where the edge network, tier two above, takes over many of the analytical and computational tasks, sorting the incoming data and only providing vetted content to the tier three cloud layer. This reduces both latency and bandwidth requirements in the network. At the same time, if communications are temporarily broken between the cloud and edge layers, the edge layer's fog computing capabilities can take over to run the tier one devices until communications can be re-established.

Complexity and Size

Today's Internet of Things is more a collection of proprietary devices, protocols, languages, and interfaces. In the future, as there is more standardization deployed, this collection will be studied as a complex system, given its fast numbers of communication links, autonomous actors, and its capacity to constantly integrate new actors. Today, however, most elements of the Internet of Things do not belong to any massive group of devices. Devices in a smart home, for example, do not communicate with anything other than the central hub of the home. These subsystems are there for reasons of privacy, reliability, and control. Only the central hub can be accessed or controlled from outside the home, meaning all sensor data, positions, and the status of the devices inside is not shared. Until such time as there is an assurance of security from more global networks about access and control of these private networks of IoT devices, and at the same time, until non-standard architectures are developed to allow the command and control of such vast numbers of internet connected devices, the IoT will likely continue as a collection of non-communicating mini-networks. SND, Software Defined Networking, appears promising in this area as a solution that can deal with the diversity and unique requirements of so many IoT applications.

For Machine Learning to take advantage of all this sensor data, ways will need to be devised to collect it into training and data sets that can be iterated over, allowing the software to learn about and be able to predict important future states of the IoT network. For the time being, unfortunately, most IoT sensor data produced in these private networks is simply being lost.

Space
Today, the question of an Internet of Thing's location in space and time has not been given priority. Smartphones, for example, allow the user to opt out of allowing an application gaining access to the phone's capacity for geolocation. In the future, the precise location, position, size, speed, and direction of every

IoT device on the network will be critical. In fact, for IoT devices to be interconnected and provide coordinated activity, the current issues of variable spatial scales, indexing for fast search and close neighbor operations, and indeed just the massive amount of data these devices will provide all have to be overcome. If the Internet of Things is to become autonomous from human-centric decision-making, then in addition to Machine Learning algorithms being used to command and coordinate them, the space and time dimensions of IoT devices will need to be addressed and standardized in a way similar to how the internet and Web have been standardized.

Jean-Louis Gassée and a "basket of remotes"

Gassée worked at Apple from 1981 to 1990 and after that was one of the founders of Be Incorporated, creator of the BeOS operating system. He describes the issue of various protocols among Internet of Things providers as the "basket of remotes" problem. As wireless remote controls gained popularity, consumers would find they ended up with a basket full of remotes — one for the TV, one for the VCR, one for the DVD player, one for the stereo, and possibly even a universal remote that was supposed to replace all the others but often failed to match at least one device. All these devices used the same technology, but because each manufacturer used a proprietary language and/or frequency to communicate with their appliance, there was no way to easily get one category of device to speak the same language as the others. In the same way, what Gassée sees happening is, as each new deployment of some Internet of Things tech reaches the consumer market, it becomes its own remote and base station, unable to communicate with other remotes or with the other base station to which other groups of IoT tech can communicate. If this state of proprietary bubbles of Internet of Things collections is not overcome, many of the perceived benefits of a vast IoT network will never be realized.

Security

Just as security is one of the main concerns for the conventional internet, security of the Internet of Things is a much-discussed topic. Many people are concerned that the industry is developing too rapidly and without an appropriate discussion about the security issues involved in these devices and their networks. The Internet of Things, in addition to standard security concerns found on the internet, has unique challenges — security controls in industry, Internet of Things businesses processes, hybrid systems, and end nodes.

Security is likely the main concern over adopting Internet of Things tech. Cyber-attacks on components of this industry are likely to increase as the scale of IoT adoption increases. And these threats are likely to become physical, as opposed to merely a virtual threat. Current Internet of Things systems has many security vulnerabilities including a lack of encrypted communication between devices, weak authentication (many devices are allowed to run in production environments with default credentials), lack of verification or encryption of software updates, and even SQL injection. These threats provide bad actors the ability to easily steal user credentials, intercept data and collect Personally Identifiable Information, or even inject malware into updated firmware.

Many internet-connected devices are already spying on people in their own homes, including kitchen appliances, thermostats, cameras, and televisions. Many components of modern cars are susceptible to manipulation should a bad actor gain access to the vehicle's onboard systems including dashboard displays, the horn, heating/cooling, hood and trunk releases, the engine, door locks, and even braking. Those vehicles with wireless connectivity are vulnerable to wireless remote attacks. Demonstration attacks on other internet-connected devices have been made as well, including cracking insulin pumps, implantable cardioverter defibrillators, and pacemakers. Because some of these devices have severe limitations on their size and processing power, they may be unable to use standard security measures like strong encryption for communication or even employing firewalls.

Privacy concerns over the Internet of Things have two main thrusts — legitimate and illegitimate uses. In legitimate uses, governments and large corporations may set up massive IoT services which by their nature collect enormous amounts of data. To a private entity, this data can be monetized in many different ways, with little or no recourse for the people whose lives and activities are swept up in the data collection. For governments, massive data collection from the Internet of Things networks provide the data necessary to provide services and infrastructure, to save resources and reduce emission, and so on. At the same time, these systems will collect enormous amounts of data on citizens, including their locations, activities, shopping habits, travel, and so on. To some, this is the realization of a true surveillance state. Without a legal framework in place to prevent governments from simply scooping up endless amounts of data to do with as they wish, it is difficult to refute this argument.

Illegitimate uses of the massive Internet of Things networks include everything from DDOS (distributed denial of service) attacks through malware attacks on one or more of the IoT devices on the network. Even more worrying, security vulnerabilities in even one device on an Internet of Things network can, by nature of the fact it is capable of full communication with all devices nearby because it has access to the encryption requirements to present itself as a legitimate device on the network, means an infected device may not only provide its illegitimate host with the data it provides, but meta data of other devices in the network, and possibly even access to the edge systems themselves.

In 2016, a DDOS attack powered by an Internet of Things device compromised by a malware infection led to over 300,000 device infections and brought down both a DNS provider and several major websites. This Mirai Botnet was able to single out for attack devices that consisted mostly of IP cameras, DVRs, printers, and routers.

While there are several initiatives being made to increase security in the Internet of Things marketplace, many argue that government regulation and inter-governmental cooperation around the world is the only way to ensure public safety.

Chapter 10:

Machine Learning and Robotics

First, we need to define a robot. They are machines, often programmable by a computer, that are able to carry out a series of complex actions without intervention. A robot can have its controls systems embedded or be controlled by an external device. In popular literature and film, many robots are designed to look like people, but in fact, they are usually designed to perform a task and that requirement determines how they appear.

Robots have been with us for almost as long as computers. George Devol invented the first digitally operated and programmable one in 1954, called Unimate. In 1961, General Motors bought it to use for lifting hot metal die castings. And like computers, robots have changed our society. Their strength, agility, and ability to continue to perfectly execute the same repetitive tasks have proved an enormous benefit. And while they did cause some serious disruption to the manufacturing industries, putting many people out of work, their ascension in our societies has provided far more employment opportunities than they have taken.

Robots in current use can be broken down into several categories:

Industrial Robots/Service Robots

These robots are probably familiar. You have likely seen them on the television or streaming video of automated factories. They usually consist of an "arm" with one or more joints, which ends with a gripper or manipulating device. They first took hold in automobile factories. They are fixed in one location and are unable to move about. Industrial robots will be found in manufacturing and industrial locations. Service robots are basically the same in design as industrial robots but are found outside of manufacturing concerns.

Educational Robots

These are robots used as teacher aids or for educational purposes on their own. As early as the 1980s, robots were introduced in classrooms with the turtles, which were used in classrooms where students could train them using the Lego programming language. There are also robot kits available for purchase like the Lego Mindstorm.

Modular Robots

Modular robots are consisted of several independent units that work together. They can be identical or have one or more variation in design. Modular robots are able to attach together to form shapes that allow them to perform tasks. The programming of modular robotic systems is of course, more complex than a single robot, but ongoing research in many universities and corporate settings is proving that this design approach is superior to single large robots for many types of applications. When combined with

Swarm Intelligence (see below), modular robots are proving quite adept at creative problem-solving.

Collaborative Robots
Collaborative robots are designed to work with human beings. They are mostly industrial robots that include safety features to ensure they do not harm anyone as they go about their assigned tasks. An excellent example of this kind of collaborative robot is Baxter. Introduced in 2012, Baxter is an industrial robot designed to be programmed to accomplish simple tasks but is able to sense when it comes into contact with a human being and stops moving.

Of course, all the examples above do not require any artificial intelligence. When robots are coupled with machine learning, researchers use the term "Robotic Learning". This field has a contemporary impact in at least four important areas:

Vision
Machine Learning has allowed robots to visually sense their environment and to make sense of what they are seeing. New items can be understood and classified without the need to program into the robot ahead of time what it is looking at.

Grasping

Coupled with vision, Machine Learning allows robots to manipulate items in their environment that they have never seen before. In the past, in an industrial factory, each time a robot was expected to interact with a different-shaped object, it would have to be programmed to know how to manipulate this new object before it could be put to work. With Machine Learning, the robot comes equipped with the ability to navigate new item shapes and sizes automatically.

Motion Control

With the aid of Machine Learning, robots are able to move about their environments and avoid obstacles in order to continue their assigned tasks.

Data

Robots are now able to understand patterns in data, both physical and logistical, and act accordingly on those patterns.

Examples of Industrial Robots and Machine Learning

One example of the benefit of applying Machine Learning to robots is of an industrial robot which receives boxes of frozen food along a conveyor. Because it is frozen, these boxes often have frost, sometimes quite a lot of frost. This actually changes the shape of the box randomly. Thus, a traditionally-trained robot with very little tolerance for these shape changes would fail to grasp the boxes correctly. With Machine Learning algorithms, the robot is now able to adapt to different shapes, random as they are and in real time, and successfully grasp the boxes.

Another industrial example includes a factory with over 90,000 different parts. It would not be possible to teach a robot how to manipulate these many items. With Machine Learning, the robot is able to be fed images of new parts it will be dealing with and it can determine its own method to manipulate them.

In 2019, there will be an estimated 2.6 million robots in service on the planet. That's up a million from

2015. As more and more robots are combined with Machine Learning algorithms, this number is sure to explode.

Chapter 11:

Machine Learning and Swarm Intelligence

Swarm Intelligence (SI) is defined as collaborative behavior, natural or artificial, of decentralized, self-organized systems. That is, Swarm Intelligence can refer to an ant colony or a "swarm" of autonomous mini-drones in a lab.

In artificial intelligence, a swarm is typically a collection of agents that interact with each other and their environment. The inspiration for Swarm Intelligence comes from nature, from the collaboration of bees to the flocking of birds to the motions of herd animals, groups of animals that appear to act intelligently even when no single individual has exceptional intelligence, and there is no centralized decision-making process.

Swarm Behavior

One of the central tenets gleaned from swarm research has been the notion of emergent behavior. When a number of individuals are given simple rules for behavior complex, behaviors seems to arise despite there being no rule or instruction to create them. Consider the artificial life program created by Craig Reynolds in 1986, which simulates bird flocking. Each individual bird was given a simple set of rules:

- avoid crowding local flockmates (separation)
- steer towards the heading average of local flockmates (alignment)
- steer to travel in the direction of the average center of local flockmates (cohesion)

When loosed, his experimental birds behaved like a real bird flock. He discovered he could add more rules to make more complex flocking behavior like goal seeking or obstacle avoidance.

Applications of Swarm Intelligence

Swarm Intelligence can be applied in many areas. Military applications include research into techniques for unmanned vehicle control. NASA is considering swarm tech for mapping planets. In a 1992 paper, George Bekey and M. Anthony Lewis discussed using swarm intelligence in nanobots inserted into the human body to attack and destroy cancer tumors.

Ant-based routing
In the telecommunication industry, the use of Swarm Intelligence has been researched using a routing table where small control packets (ants) are rewarded for successfully traversing a route. Variations on this research include forwards, backward, and bi-directional rewards. Such systems are not repeatable because they behave randomly, so commercial uses have thus far proved elusive.

One promising application for Swarm Intelligence is wireless communication networks. In this case, the network relies on a limited number of locations that are expected to provide adequate coverage for users. In this case, the application of a different kind of ant-based swarm intelligence, stochastic diffusion search (SDS) has modeled this problem with great success.

Airlines have experimented with ant-based Swarm Intelligence. Southwest Airlines uses software that employs swarm theory to manage its airlines on the ground. Each pilot acts like an "ant" in the swarm, discovering through experience what gate is best for him or her. This behavior turns out to be the best for the airline as well. The pilot colony uses the gates each one is familiar with and so can arrive at and leave from quickly, with the software providing feedback should a particular gate or route be predicted to suffer a back-up.

Crowd Simulation
The movies are using Swarm Intelligence simulations for depicting animal and human crowds. In Batman Returns, Swarm Intelligence was employed to create a realistic bat simulation. For The Lord of the Rings movies, Swarm Intelligence simulations were employed to depict the massive battle scenes.

Human Swarms

When combined with mediating software, a network of distributed people can be organized into swarms by implementing closed-loop, real-time control systems. These systems, acting out in real-time, allow human actors to act in a unified manner, a collective intelligence that operates like a single mind, making predictions or answering questions. Testing in academic settings suggests these human swarms can out-perform individuals in a wide variety of real-world situations.

Swarm Intelligence and Machine Intelligence are both forms of artificial intelligence. It's debatable whether Swarm Intelligence is a sub-set of Machine Intelligence. It is a different approach toward the goal of smart machines, modeling the behavior of particular kinds of animals to achieve desired results. But however they are classified, Swarm Intelligence and Machine Intelligence can complement each other. In an attempt to determine emotions from a text, a Swarm Intelligence approach will differ from a monolithic approach. Instead of one Machine Learning algorithm to detect emotion in text, a swarm approach might be to create many simple Machine

Learning algorithms, each designed to detect a single emotion. These heuristics can be layered in hierarchies to avoid any emotion-detector fouling up the end result. Let's look at an example. Imagine a Machine Learning swarm meant to detect emotion in written text examining this sentence: "When I pulled back the covers of my bed this morning, a giant spider ran over my leg and I ran out of the bedroom screaming."

This is a complex sentence and very difficult for natural language Machine Learning algorithms to parse for emotion. However, a swarm of simple Machine Learning algorithms dedicated to detecting one kind of emotion would likely have the terror algorithm scoring high, while fun and happiness scored low.

So far our imaginary system is working well. But take a more difficult example:

"I watched the game yesterday and saw us kick butt in the first period, but by the third, I was terrified we would lose."

Human beings understand the hyperbole. The writer is not terrified but anxious the team will lose the game. Our swarm Machine Intelligence algorithms could have the fear/terror algorithm scoring high, but this would be inaccurate. Because swarm models can be hierarchical, one model's output could be the input of another. In this case, a master model that detects emotion could filter through the outputs of each individual emotion algorithm, noting that "excitement" had been triggered by "kick butt", parse that the subject of the sentence is a sport and determine that anxiety is a better fit than terror.

It seems fair to define Swarm Intelligence as an application of Machine Learning with an extremely narrow focus.

Chapter 12:

Machine Learning Models

There are many models of Machine Learning. These theoretical describe the heuristics used to accomplish the ideal, allowing the machine to learn on their own. Below is a list and description of some of the most popular.

Decision Tree
Just about everyone has used the decision tree technique. Either formally or informally, we decide on a single course of action from many possibilities based on previous experience. The possibilities look like branches and we take one of them and reject the others.

The decision tree model gets its name from the shape created when its decision processes are drawn out graphically. A decision tree offers a great deal of flexibility in terms of what input values it can receive. As well, a tree's outputs can take the form of a category, binary, or numerical. Another strength of decision trees is how the degree of influence of different input variables can be determined by the level of decision node in which they are considered.

A weakness of decision trees is the fact that every decision boundary is a forced binary split. There is no nuance. Each decision is either yes or no, one or zero. As well, the decision criteria can consider only a single variable at a time. There cannot be a combination of more than one input variable.

Decision trees cannot be updated incrementally. That is to say, once a tree has been trained on a training set, it must be thrown out and a new one created to tackle new training data.

Ensemble Methods address many tree limitations. In essence, the ensemble method uses more than one tree to increase output accuracy. There are two main ensemble methods — bagging and boosting.

The bagging ensemble method (known as Bootstrap Aggregation) is mean to reduce decision tree variance. The training data is broken up randomly into subsets and each subset is used to train a decision tree. The results from all trees are averaged, providing a more robust predictive accuracy than any single tree on its own.

The boosting ensemble method resembles a multi-stage rocket. The main booster of a rocket supplies the vehicle with a large amount of inertia. When its fuel is spent, it detaches and the second stage combines its acceleration to the inertia already imparted to the rocket and so on. For decision trees, the first tree operates on the training data and produces its outputs. The next tree uses the earlier tree's output as its input. When the input is in error the weighting it is given, makes it more likely the next tree will identify and at least partially mitigate this error. The end result of the run is a strong learner emerging from a series of weaker learners.

Linear Regression

The premise of linear regression methods rests on the assumption that the output (numeric value) may be expressed as a combination of the input variable set (also numeric). A simple example might look like this:

x = a1y1, a2y2, a3y3...

Where x is the output, a1...an are the weights accorded to each input, and y1...yn are the inputs.

The strength of a linear regression model lies in the fact it can produce well in terms of scores and performance. It is also capable of incremental learning.

A weakness of the linear regression model is the fact that it assumes linear input features, which might not be the case. Inputs must be tested mathematically for linearity.

K-Means Clustering Algorithm

K-means is an unsupervised machine learning algorithm for cluster analysis. It is an iterative, non-deterministic method. The algorithm operates on data sets using predefined clusters. You can think of clusters like categories. For example, consider K-Means Clustering on a set of search results. The search term "jaguar" returns all pages containing the word Jaguar. But the word "Jaguar" has more than one classification. It can refer to a type of car, it can refer to an operating system created by the Apple Computers, and it can refer to the animal. K-Means clustering algorithms can be used to group results that talk about similar concepts. So, the algorithm will group all results that discuss jaguar as an animal into one cluster, discussions of Jaguar as a car into another cluster, and discussions of Jaguar as an operating system into a third. And so on.

K-Means Clustering Applications

K-Means Clustering algorithms are used by most web search engines to cluster web pages by similarity and to identify the relevance of search results. But in any application where unstructured data needs to be divided into meaningful categories, K-Means Clustering is a valuable tool to accomplish this task.

Neural Network

We have covered neural networks in detail above. The strengths of neural networks are their ability to learn non-linear relationships between inputs and outputs.

Bayesian Network

Bayesian networks produce probabilistic relationships between outputs and inputs. This type of network requires all data to be binary. The strengths of the Bayesian network include high scalability and support for incremental learning. We discussed Bayesian models in more detail earlier in the book. In particular, this Machine Learning method is particularly good at classification tasks such as detecting if an email is or is not spam.

Support Vector Machine

Support Vector Machine algorithms are supervised Machine Learning algorithms that can be used for classification and regression analysis, although they are most often used for classification problems and so we will focus on those.

Support Vector Machines work by dividing categories using a hyperplane (basically a flat sheet in 3 dimensions). On one side of the hyperplane will be one category, on the other side the other category. This works well if the categories to be separated are clearly divisible, but what if they overlap? Imagine a series of blue and red dots spread out randomly within a square. There is nowhere to place a hyperplane between the blue and red dots because they overlap each other on the two-dimensional sheet.

Support Vector Machines deal with this problem by mapping the data into a higher dimension. Imagine these dots being lifted into the air in a cube, where the red dots are "heavier" than the blue dots, and therefore remain closer to the bottom and the blue dots closer to the top. If there is still an overlap, the Support Vector Machine algorithm maps them into yet another dimension, until a clear separation appears and the two categories of dots can be separated by the hyperplane.

This is an incredibly powerful method for classifying data, but there are issues, of course. One is the fact that looking at the data once it has been mapped into higher dimensions isn't possible. It has become gibberish. Support Vector Machines are sometimes referred to as black boxes for this reason. As well, Support Vector Machine training times can be high, so this algorithm isn't as well suited to very large data sets, as the larger the data set, the longer the training required.

Chapter 13:

Applications of Machine Learning

You are probably using real-world applications of Machine Learning every day. Below is a sample of just some of the ways Machine Learning is being used today in our world. Some are easily recognized, others are hidden and operating the background, making our lives easier, or more convenient, or even safer.

Virtual Personal Assistants

Google Assistant, Apple's Siri, Amazon Alexa, Microsoft's Cortana – these are just a few of the virtual assistants we interact with almost every day. These are probably the most popular and well-known examples of applied Machine Learning. When you use these personal assistants, there is more than one kind of Machine Learning working behind the scenes. First, you can speak to them using ordinary language and they answer back the same way. Speech recognition is a Machine Learning skill these assistants use to understand you. Then, of course, once they have recognized what you said and understood what you are asking for, they usually use yet more Machine Learning to search for answers to your questions. Finally, they respond with answers and track your response, compare it to previous responses, and use all this data to be more accurate and efficient for your future requests.

Commuting Predictions

If you've used Google or Apple maps, you've used Machine Learning to get yourself to your destination. These apps store our location, direction, and speed in a central location to lead you to your destination, providing turn details and so on before you actually reach the turning point. At the same time, they are aggregating the data from all of the users nearby who are using their service and using all this information to predict and track traffic congestion and to modify your route in real-time to avoid it. When there are not enough people using the app at any given time, the system relies on predictive Machine Learning from previous traffic data from different days at the same location to anticipate the traffic if it is unable to collect in real-time.

Uber and Lyft also rely on Machine Learning to decide on the cost of a ride, basing their decisions on current demand, as well as predictions concerning rider demand at any given time. These services would become technically impossible without Machine Learning crunching massive amounts of data, both historical and in real-time.

Online Fraud Detection

Securing cyberspace is one of the many goals of Machine Learning. Tracking online fraud is an important tool for achieving this goal. PayPal employs Machine Learning in its efforts to prevent money laundering. Their software can track the millions of transactions taking place and separate legitimate from illegitimate transactions going on between buyers and sellers.

Data Security

Another form of security in cyberspace is combating malware. This is a massive problem and getting worse. 1 in 13 web requests lead to malware on the internet today in 2018, and that's up 3% from 2016. The problem is so vast only something as powerful as Machine Learning is able to cope. Fortunately, most new malware is really just older malware with minor changes. This is something Machine Learning can search for quickly and with a high degree of accuracy, meaning new malware is caught almost as quickly as it can be created.

Machine Learning is also very good at monitoring data access and finding anomalies, which might predict possible security breaches.

Personal Security

Long line at the airport? Taking forever to get into that concert? Those long lines are for your security. Everyone getting on a plane or entering a large event is screened to ensure the safety of the flight or event. Machine Learning is starting to provide assistance to the manual checking of people, spotting anomalies human screenings might miss, and helping to prevent false alarms. This help promises to speed up security screening in a substantial way, while at the same time ensuring safer events through the more powerful screening processes Machine Learning can provide.

Video Surveillance

How many movies have you watched where a video feed is interrupted with a loop of a parade or cell, so the good guys (or bad guys) can move through the monitored area without being seen? Well, Machine Learning may not be able to defeat this tactic any better than the hapless security guards in the movies, but it is able to take over a lot of the drudgery of monitoring live video feeds. The benefit is Machine Learning never gets tired, or needs a break, or has its attention wander so nothing is ever missed. Machine learning can focus on anomalous behavior like standing for a long time without moving, sleep on benches, or stumbling, meaning human beings can be freed up to do what they do much better, deal with these people as required.

Social Media Services

Social media platforms utilize many forms of Machine Learning. If you've been using these platforms, then you've been using Machine Learning. Facebook, for example, constantly offers you friend suggestions of "people you may know." This is a simple concept of learning through experience. Facebook's technology watches who your friends are (and who those friend's friends are), what profiles you visit, and how often, what articles you follow, and pages you visit. By aggregating this information, the Machine Learning is able to provide people you are likely to enjoy interacting with and so recommends them to you as Friend suggestions.

Or when you upload a picture to Facebook of yourself and some friends, Facebook use Machine Learning to identify those people in your photo by comparing them to images your friends have uploaded of themselves. But this is not all. These photos are scanned for the poses people are making, as well as any unique features in the background, Geo-locating the image if it can.

Online Customer Support
Many websites offer a service to text chat with customer service while you browse their pages. You've probably chatted with one or more of them. But what you might not know is, not all of those text chats are with real people. Many companies cannot afford to pay a person to provide this service, so instead a chatbot will answer your questions, itself relying on details from the website to provide its answers.

Machine Learning means these chatbots get better over time, learning how and how not to answer questions, and to seem more human in their interactions.

Search Engine Results, Refined

Search engine providers, from Google on down, rely on Machine Learning to refine their responses to search terms. They monitor your activity after you've been given some results to examine. Do you click on the first link and stay on this page for a long time? Then their results to your query were probably good. Or do you navigate to page 2 or 3 or further down the results they have provided, clicking some links and immediately returning? This means the results returned did not satisfy your query as well as they could. Machine Learning uses this feedback to improve the search algorithms used.

Product Recommendations/Market Personalization

Have you ever been shopping online for something you didn't intend to buy? Or were considering buying, but not for a while? So you look online at a product, maybe at the same product in more than one online store. Comparing prices, customer review, and so on. You might even put one of them in your shopping cart to checkout taxes and shipping fees. Then you close these tabs and get back to work.

Over the next few days, you realize you're seeing this product and similar products all over web pages you visit. Advertisements for the product seem to be everywhere for the next few days. And this is just the tip of the iceberg.

Using the kind of information gathered from your shopping/browsing practices, Machine Learning is used to tailor everything from specific email campaigns aimed at you personally, to similar product advertisements, to coupons or deals by the retailers offering the product you'd been looking at. As the amount of data for these Machine Learning algorithms grows, expect this personal approach to advertising to become even more focused and accurate.

Financial Trading
Being able to "predict the market" is something of a holy grail in financial circles. The truth is, humans

have never been much better at this than chance. However, Machine Learning is bringing the grail within the human grasp. Using the power of massive supercomputers crunching enormous quantities of data, large financial firms with proprietary predictive systems make a large volume, high-speed transactions. With high speed and enough volume, even low probability trades can end up making these firms enormous amounts of money. And those of us who can't afford massive supercomputers? We're better off doing our stock trading the old-fashioned way — research specific companies and invest in businesses with solid business plans and room in the market for growth. No doubt one day soon there will be a Machine Learning algorithm to manage this for you.

Healthcare

Machine Learning is revolutionizing the health care system. With its ability to ingest enormous amounts of data and use that to spot patterns human simply cannot see, Machine Learning is able to diagnose some diseases up to a year before a human diagnosis. At the same time, by crunching large data sets of populations, Machine Learning is able to identify groups or individuals who are more likely to need hospitalization due to diseases like diabetes. The predictive power of Machine Learning is likely the most fruitful avenue in healthcare since much of disease-fighting rests on early diagnosis.

Another inroad to healthcare by Machine Learning is robotic assistants in the operating room. While many of these robots are simply tools used by doctors, some are semi-autonomous and aid in the surgery themselves. In the not too distant future, Machine Learning will allow robot surgeons to perform operations with complete autonomy. This will free up surgeons to perform the far more complex and experimental procedures that Machine Learning is not prepared to perform.

Natural Language Processing
Being able to understand natural human speech has been a long time coming. We've been talking to our robots in movies and cartoons for more than 70 years. And now, thanks to Machine Learning, that ability is being realized all around us. We can talk to our smartphones and we can talk to a company's "customer support" robot and tell it what we need

help with. Natural language processing is even able to take complex legal contract language and translate it into plain language for non-lawyers to understand.

Smart Cars

The autonomous car is very close. But it won't just be autonomous, it will be smart. It will interconnect with other cars and other internet-enabled devices, as well as learn about its owner and passengers, providing internal adjustments to the temperature, audio, seat settings, and so on. Because autonomous cars will communicate with each other as they become more numerous on the road, they will become safer. Accidents will drop to next to zero when people are no longer behind the wheel. This is the power of Machine Learning really flexing its muscles, and only one of the many, many ways it will change our human future.

Chapter 14:

Programming and (Free) Datasets

For those interested in the world of programming in Machine Learning, there are many, many resources on the web. This chapter will identify and describe some excellent free data sets available for download and use in Machine Learning programs, as well as suggest an option for learning beginning level Machine Learning software development using the Python programming language.

Data Sets

As we've learned, the most difficult part of using data sets to train Machine Learning algorithms, aside from acquiring the data itself, is to prepare it for supervised learning. The data sets listed below are all labeled appropriately for their subject matter, so all you need to do is download them and make them available for your software to work with.

MINIST database of handwritten digits:
http://yann.lecun.com/exdb/mnist/
This database includes a training set of 60,000 and a test set of 10,000 samples of hand-written digits (0-9) by hundreds of different people. This set is valuable to design a Machine Learning algorithm capable of "reading" hand-written text.
There is an online JavaScript implementation of this dataset available for you to see how it might work for you: http://myselph.de/neuralNet.html

ABC (Australian Broadcasting Corporation) One Million Headlines:
https://www.kaggle.com/therohk/million-headlines/home

This database includes over one million headlines from the Australian Broadcast Corporation published on their website from February 19, 2003 to December 31, 2017. This data set lends itself to an unstructured Machine Learning algorithm.

Released under CC0: Public Domain,

https://creativecommons.org/publicdomain/zero/1.0

COCO (Common Objects in Context):

http://cocodataset.org/

Large-scale image detection and segmentation dataset.

Released under Creative Commons Attribution 4.0 License,

https://creativecommons.org/licenses/by/4.0/legalcode

ImageNet:

http://www.image-net.org

1.5 million images with class labels and multiple bounding boxes

Open Images Dataset:

https://storage.googleapis.com/openimages/web/index.html

Offers a training set of more than 9 million images

Large Movie Review Dataset (from IMDB.com):
http://ai.stanford.edu/~amaas/data/sentiment/
50,000 movie reviews from IMDB.com, half in training and half in testing.
Include additional 50,000 unlabeled reviews for unsupervised learning.

Online Machine Learning Resources

Python is a very popular yet powerful interpreted language. Below are two beginner-level Machine Learning examples you can download and run on your computer. They come with access to sample data sets, but with some time and effort could be modified to deal with other data sets like those provided above.

One of the benefits of decades of development in Machine Learning is many algorithms have been boxed up for use by anyone. This means people can deploy them on data sets without having to know the detailed mathematics behind how they function. The disadvantage with this approach is while you can use such packaged Machine Learning algorithms without knowing the math behind them, the results you achieve will be limited to what the unmodified algorithm can achieve on its own. In order to achieve better results, you will need to edit the algorithm itself.

Your First Machine Learning Project in Python Step-By-Step

https://machinelearningmastery.com/machine-learning-in-python-step-by-step/

This course will walk you through every step you need to run your own Machine Learning algorithm. The tutorial is in two parts — how to acquire and get started in python and then how to create your first Machine Learning project using python.

Practical Machine Learning Tutorial with Python Introduction

https://pythonprogramming.net/machine-learning-tutorial-python-introduction/

This is a more advanced course using python to run Machine Learning algorithms. It assumes you have some familiarity with python, so until you have some experience with python, this tutorial might not be the best to start with.

Chapter 15:

Limitations of Machine Learning

There are many problems and limitations with Machine Learning. This chapter will go over the technical issues that are currently or may in the future limit the development of Machine Learning. Finally, it will end with some philosophical concerns about possible issues Machine Learning may bring about in the future.

Concerns about Machine Learning limitations have been summarized in a simple phrase, which outlines the main objects to Machine Learning. It suggests Machine Learning is Greedy, Brittle, Opaque and Shallow. Let's examine each one in turn.

Greedy
By greedy, critics of Machine Learning point to the need for massive amounts of training data is available

in order to successfully train Machine Learning systems to acceptable levels of error. Because Machine Learning systems are trained not programmed, their usefulness will be directly proportional to the amount (and quality) of the data sets used to train them. At the same time, the processing power required to crunch such massive amounts of data limits access to Machine Learning strategies to only the wealthiest corporations and governments.

Related to the size of training data required is the fact that, for supervised and semi-supervised Machine Learning training, the raw data used for training must first be labeled so that it can be meaningfully employed by the software to train. In essence, the task of labeling training data means to clean up the raw content and prepare it for the software to ingest. But labeling data can itself be a very complex task, as well as often a laborious and tedious one. None or improperly labeled data fed into a supervised Machine Learning system will produce nothing of value. It will just be a waste of time.

Brittle

To say Machine Learning is brittle is to highlight a very real and difficult problem in Artificial Intelligence. The problem is, even after a Machine Learning system has been trained to provide extremely accurate and valuable predictions on data it has been trained to deal with, asking that trained system to examine a data set even slightly different from the type it was trained on will often cause a complete failure of the system to produce any predictive value. That is to say, Machine Learning systems are unable to contextualize what they have learned and apply it to even extremely similar circumstances to those on which they have been trained. At the same time, attempting to train an already trained Machine Learning algorithm with a different data set will cause the system to "forget" its previous learning, losing, in turn, all the time and effort put in to preparing the previous data sets and training the algorithm with it.

Bias in Machine Learning systems is another example of how Machine Learning systems can be brittle. In fact, there are several different kinds of bias that threaten Artificial Intelligence. Here are a few:

Bias in Data:

Machine Learning is, for the foreseeable future at least, at the mercy of the data used to train it. If this data is biased in any way, whether deliberately or by accident, those biases hidden within it may be passed onto the Machine Learning system itself. If not caught during the training stage, this bias can taint the work of the system when it is out in the real world doing what it was designed to do. Facial recognition provides a good example, where facial recognition systems trained in predominantly white environments with predominantly white samples of faces, have trouble recognizing people with non-white facial pigmentation.

Acquired Bias:

It is sometimes the case that, while interacting with people in the real world, Machine Learning systems can acquire the biases of the people they are exposed to. A real-world example was Microsoft's Tay, a chatbot designed to interact with people on Twitter using natural language. Within 24 hours, Tay became a pretty foul troll spouting racists and misogynist statements. Microsoft pulled the plug (and set about white-washing twitter). Many of the truly offensive things Tay said were the result of people telling it to say them (there was an option to tell Tay to repeat a phrase you sent it), but there were some very troubling comments produced by Tay that it was not instructed to repeat. Microsoft was clearly aware of how nasty Twitter can get and I think it's fair to say creating a racist, misogynist chatbot was just about the last thing on their whiteboard. So if a massive, wealthy company like Microsoft cannot train an artificial intelligence that doesn't jump into the racist, woman-hating camp of nasty internet trolls, what does that say about the dangers inherent in any artificial intelligence system we create to interact in the real-world with real people?

Emergent Bias:

An echo chamber is a group or collection of people who all believe the same things. This could be a political meeting in a basement or a chatroom on the internet. Echo chambers are not tolerant of outside ideas, especially those that disagree with or attempt to refute the group's core beliefs. Facebook has become, in many ways, the preeminent echo chamber producer on Earth. But while the echo chamber phrase is meant to describe a group of people with similar ideas, Facebook's artificial intelligence has taken this idea one step further: to an echo chamber of one. The Machine Learning system Facebook deploys to gather newsfeeds and other interesting bits of information to show to you can become just such an echo chamber. As the artificial intelligence learns about your likes and dislikes, about your interests and activities, it begins to create a bubble around you that, while it might seem comforting, will not allow opposing or offensive views to reach you. The area where this is most alarming is news and information. Being constantly surrounded by people who agree with you, reading news that only confirms your beliefs, is not necessarily a good thing. How we know we are correct about a particular issue is by testing our beliefs against who believe otherwise. Do our arguments hold up to their criticism or might we be wrong? In a Facebook echo chamber of one, that kind of learning and growth becomes less and less possible. Some studies suggest that spending time with people who agree with you tends to polarize groups, making the divisions between them worse.

Goals Conflict Bias:

Machine Learning can often support and reinforce biases that exist in the real world because doing so increases their reward system (a system is "rewarded" when it achieves a goal). For example, imagine you run a college and you want to increase enrollment. One of the things you might do is to advertise on social media sites and other places on the internet. The contract you have with the advertising company is that you will pay a certain amount for each click you get, meaning someone has seen your advertisement for the college and was interested enough to at least click on the link to see what you are offering. Of course, a simple generic ad like "Go to College!" wouldn't work so well, so you run several ads simultaneously, offering degrees in engineering, teaching, mathematics, and nursing.

It is in the advertiser's best interest to get as many clicks to your landing pages as possible. So they employ a Machine Learning algorithm to track who clicks on what advertisement, and it begins to target those groups with the specific ads to gain more clicks. So far, from the outside, this seems like a win-win. The advertiser is making more revenue and your college is receiving more potential students examining your courses. But then you notice something in the aggregate data of link clicks. Most of the clicks you are receiving for math and engineering are from young men, while most of the clicks for nursing and teaching are young women. This aligns with an unfortunate cultural stereotype that still exists in western culture and your college is perpetuating it. In its desire to be rewarded, the Machine Learning assigned maximizing click for your advertising campaign found an existing social bias and exploited it to increase revenue for its owner. These two goals, increasing your enrollment and reducing gender bias in employment, have come into conflict and Machine Learning sacrificed one to achieve the other.

Opaque

One of the main criticisms of Machine Learning, and in particular, against Neural Networks, is that they are unable to explain to their creators why they arrive at the decisions they do. This is a problem for two reasons: one, more and more countries are adopting internet laws that include a right to an explanation. The most influential of these laws is the GDPR (The EU General Data Protection Regulation), which guarantees EU citizens the right to an explanation why an algorithm that deals with an important part of their lives made the decision it did. For example, an EU citizen turned down for a loan by a Machine Learning algorithm has a right to demand why this happened. Because some artificial intelligence tools like neural networks are often not capable of providing any explanation for their decision, and the fact this decision is hidden in layers of math not readily available for human examination, such an explanation may not be possible. This has in fact slowed down adoption of artificial intelligence in some areas. The second reason it is important that artificial intelligence be able to explain its decisions to its creators is for verifying that the underlying process is in fact meeting expectations in the real world. For Machine Learning, the decision-making process is mathematical and probabilistic. In the real world, decisions often need to be confirmed by the reasoning used to achieve them.

Take, for example, a self-driving car involved in an accident. Assuming the hardware of the car is not completely destroyed, experts will want to know why the car took the actions it did. Perhaps there is a court case and the decision of liability rests on how and why the car took the actions it did. Without transparency around the decision-making process of the software, justice might not be served in the courts, software engineers may not be able to find and correct flaws, and more people might be in danger from the same software running in different cars.

The Philosophical Objections: Jobs, Evil, and Taking Over the World

Jobs:

One of the main concerns surrounding artificial intelligence is the way these systems are encroaching upon human employment. Automation is not a new problem, and vast numbers of jobs have already been lost in manufacturing and other such industries to robots and automated systems. Because of this, some argue that this concern that machines and artificial intelligence will take over so many jobs there will be no more economy is not really a threat. We've encountered such takeovers before, but the economy shifted and people found other jobs. In fact, some argue that the net number of jobs has increased since the loss of so many jobs to automation. So what's the problem?

The problem is this next round of job losses will be unprecedented. Artificial Intelligence will not only replace drudgery and danger. It will keep going. One of the largest employment groups in the United States is a professional truck driver. There are 3.5 million of them currently. How long until all trucking is handled by Machine Learning systems running self-driving trucks? And what about ride sharing services like Uber and Lyft?

The question to ask is not what jobs will be replaced, but what jobs can't be replaced. In the Machine Learning round of employment disruption, white collar jobs are just as much in jeopardy as blue. Accountants, financial advisers, copywriters, and advertisers. Can you imagine more than a handful of tasks that machines won't be able to do in 10 years? How about 20?

The pro-artificial intelligence camp argues that this disruption will open up new kinds of jobs, things we can't even imagine. And in a way, they may be right. Each major disruption of the economy in the past that displaced many forms of employment with automation often caused the creation of new employment unforeseen before the disruption. The difference with artificial intelligence is, there is no reason to believe these new forms of employment won't quickly be taken over by Machine Learning systems as well.

And all the above assumes the use of the current type of very specific Machine Learning. What happens if researchers are able to generalize learning in artificial intelligence? What if these systems become able to generalize what they learn and apply what they know in new and different contexts? Such a generalized artificial intelligence system could very quickly learn to do just about anything.

Evil:
A very serious danger from artificial intelligence is the fact that anyone with resources can acquire and use it. Western governments are already toying with the idea of autonomous weapons platforms using artificial intelligence to engage and defeat an enemy, with little or no human oversight. As frightening as this might be, in these countries at least, there are checks and balances on the development and deployment of such devices, and in the end, a population that can vote for or against such things.

But even if these platforms are developed and only used appropriately, what is to stop an enemy from capturing one, reverse engineering it, and then developing their own? What's to stop a rival power from investing in the infrastructure to create their own?

The threat of Machine Learning used by bad actors is very real. How do we control who gains access to this powerful technology? The genie is out of the bottle. It can't be put back in. So how do we keep it from falling into the wrong hands?

Taking Over the World:
Finally, we'll take a look at the end humanity caused by super intelligent machines. Luminaries such as Steven Hawking and Elon Musk have quite publicly voiced their concerns about the dangers artificial intelligence could post to humanity. In the *Terminator* movie franchise, a Defense Department artificial intelligence called Skynet, tasked with protecting the United States, determined that human beings, everywhere, were the real threat. Using its control of the US nuclear arsenal, it launched an attack on Russia, which precipitated a global nuclear war. In the disaster that followed, it began systematically wiping out the human race.

This example is extreme and probably better as a movie plot than something we have to worry about from artificial intelligence in the real world. No, the danger to humanity from artificial intelligence lies more likely in a paperclip factory.

Imagine an automated paperclip factory run by an artificial intelligence system capable of learning over time. This system is smarter than human beings. It has one goal — produce as many paperclips as possible, as efficiently as possible. Sounds harmless enough. And at first, it is. The system learns everything there is to know about creating a paperclip, from the mining of metals, smelting, transportation of raw steel to its factory, the automated factory floor, clip design specifications, and so on.

As it learns over time, however, it runs up against walls it cannot surpass. A factory can only be so efficient. Eventually boosting efficiency further becomes impossible. Acquiring the supply chain from mining to smelting to transportation might come next. But again, once these aspects of the business are acquired and streamlined, they no longer offer a path to the goal — increase production and efficiency.

As artificial intelligence collects more information about the world, it comes to learn how to take over other factories, retool them for paperclip production, and increase output. Then more transportation, mining, and smelting might need to be acquired. After a few more factories are retrofitted, the distribution center where the paperclips are delivered begins to fill with paperclips. There are many more than anyone needs. But this is not the concern of our artificial intelligence. The supply side of the paperclip chain is not part of its programming.

It learns about politics and so begins to influence elections when people try to stop paperclip production. It continues to acquire and take over businesses and technologies to increase production.

Absurd as it sounds (and this is just a thought experiment), imagine the entire Earth, now devoid of people, a massive mining, transportation, smelting, and paperclip production facility. And as the piles of unwanted, unused paperclips turn into mountains to rival the stone ones of our planet, with metal resources dwindling, our stalwart AI turns its lenses up to see the moon, Mars, the asteroid belt. It sees other solar systems, other galaxies, and finally the universe. So much raw metal out there. All just waiting to be made into paperclips...

Chapter 16:

Machine Learning and the Future

After the previous chapter, it's probably best to end on a positive note, by an examination of the positive future of Machine Learning. This chapter will break down the future of Machine Learning into segments of society and the economy in an effort to put these possible futures in a useful context.

Security

Facial recognition, aberrant behavior detection, these toolkits from Machine Learning is available today. They will become ubiquitous in the future, protecting the public from criminal behavior and getting people in trouble the help they need.

But what about the other Machine Learning security features in the future?

In the cyber world, Machine Learning will grow and increase its influence in identifying cyber-attacks, malicious software code, and unexpected communication attempts. At the same time, dark hat software crackers are also working on Machine Learning tools to aid them in breaking into networks, accessing private data, and causing service disruptions. The future of the cyber world will be an ongoing war between White and Black Hat Machine Learning tools. Who will win? We hope the White Hat Machine Learning algorithms will be victorious but win or lose, the battle will slowly move out of the hands of people and into the algorithms of Machine Learning.

Another sweeping change to security we might see in the near future is autonomous drones controlled by Machine Learning algorithms. Drones can maintain constant aerial surveillance over entire cities at very little cost. With advancements in image recognition, motion capture, video recognition, and natural language processing, they will be able to communicate with people on the street, response to natural disasters and automobile accidents, ferry medications needed in emergency situations where traditional service vehicles cannot access, and find and rescue lost hikers by leading them to safety, deliver them needed supplies, and alerting authorities of their GPS location.

Markets

The rise of Machine Learning will generate completely new Artificial Intelligence-based products and services. Entire industries will be created to service this new software, as well as new products to be added to the Internet of Things, including a new generation of robots complete with learning algorithms and the ability to see, hear, and communicate with us using natural language.

Retail

In the retail sector, we will see enhanced and more accurate personalization. But instead of merely showing us what we want, Machine Learning will be dedicated to showing us what we need. Perhaps we've been eating too much fast food this week. A smart algorithm looking out for our well-being would not throw more and more fast food ads in our face, instead, reminders about our health, coupons for gym memberships, or recipes for our favorite salads might become part of the Artificial Intelligence toolkit for our notifications. Machine Learning will help us to balance our lives in many ways by using knowledge about general health, and our own medical records, to provide information about not only what we want, but also what we might need.

Healthcare

Machine Learning will know almost everything about us and not only through records on the internet. When we visit our doctor to complain about a sore shoulder, Machine Learning might inform our GP about how we are prone to slouch at work, possibly altering the doctor's diagnosis from a prescription for analgesics to a prescription to exercises to do at work, as well as some tutoring on better sitting posture.

On the diagnostic side, Machine Learning will do the busy work it is best at: examining our x-rays and blood-work and mammograms, looking for patterns human beings cannot see, getting pre-emptive diagnostic information to our doctors so we can head off serious illness at early stages, or perhaps before it even happens. Doctors will be freed up to spend time with their patients, providing the human touch so often missing in medicine.

Many if not most surgeries will be performed by Artificial Intelligence-enabled robots, either assisting human surgeons, being supervised by them, or even, eventually, working fully autonomously. Machine Learning will monitor our blood gasses under anesthesia, our heart rate and other health measures during operations, and reaction in milliseconds should something appear to be wrong. Iatrogenic disease will decrease dramatically, if not disappear completely.

The Environment and Sustainability
Machine Learning will be able to study the movement

of people in cities. What they use and don't use, their patterns of use, how they travel, and where. Deep Learning from this data will allow city planners to employ Machine Learning algorithms to design and construct both more efficient and pleasant cities. It will allow massive increases in density without sacrificing quality of life. These efficiencies will reduce, possibly eliminate net carbon emissions from cities.

Augmented Reality

When we wear about Google (or Microsoft or Apple or Facebook) glasses in the future, the embedded processes, video capture, audio capture, and microphones on these devices will do much more than give us directions to find a location. Machine Learning will be able to see what we see and provide explanations and predictive guidance throughout our day. Imagine having your day "painted" with relevant information on interior walls and doors, and outside on buildings and signs, guiding you through your schedule with the information you need right when you need it.

Information Technology

Machine Learning will become a tool people and businesses can apply as needed like SasS. This MLaaS will allow software to be aware of its surroundings, to see us, to hear us, and speak to us in natural language. Connected to the internet, every device will become smart, and generate an ecosphere around us that attends to our needs and concerns, often before we even realize we have them. These "Cognitive Services" will provide APIs and SDKs, leading to rapid "smart" software development and deployment.

Specialized hardware will increase the speed of Machine Learning training, as well as increase its speed in servicing us. Dedicated AI chips will bring about a sea change in Artificial Intelligence speed and ubiquity.

Microcomputers will come equipped with Machine Learning capabilities so that even the smallest device will be able to understand its surroundings. Where there is no convenient power supply, these devices will run on dime-sized batteries, lasting for months or years of service before needing replacement. Currently, these microcomputers cost about 50 cents each. This price will drop. They will be deployed practically everywhere.

Quantum computing and Machine Learning will merge, bringing solutions to problems we don't even know we have yet.

We will see the rise of intelligent robots of every size, make and description, all dedicated to making our lives better.

Trust Barriers

Natural speech means we will be able to talk to our devices and be understood by them. The current trust barriers between some people, business sectors, and governments will slowly break down as Machine Learning demonstrates its reliability and effectiveness. Improved unsupervised learning will reduce the time required to develop new Machine Learning software with required specifications.

Conclusion

Thank you for making it through to the end of *Machine Learning for Beginners*. Let's hope it was informative and able to provide you with all of the information you needed to begin to understand this extensive topic.

The impact of Machine Learning on our world is already ubiquitous. Our cars, our phones, our houses, and so much more are already being controlled and maintained through rudimentary Machine Learning systems. But in the future, Machine Learning will radically change the world. Some of those changes are easy to predict. In the next decade or two, people will no longer drive cars, instead, automated cars will drive people. But in many other ways, the effect of Machine Learning on our world is difficult to predict. Will Machine Learning algorithms replace so many jobs, from trucking to accounting, to many other disciplines, that there won't be much work left for people? In 100 years, will there be work for anyone at all? We don't know the answer to questions like this because there is so far no limit to what Machine

Learning can accomplish, given time and data and the will to use it to achieve a particular task.

The future is not necessarily frightening. If there is no work in the future, it won't mean that things aren't getting done. Food will still be grown, picked, transported to market, and displayed in stores. It's just that people won't have to do any of that labor. As a matter of fact, stores won't be necessary either, since the food we order can be delivered directly to our homes. What will the world be like if human beings have almost unlimited leisure time? Is this a possible future?

The only real certainty about artificial intelligence and Machine Learning is that it is increasing in both speed of deployment and in areas which it can influence. It promises many benefits and many radical changes in our society.

Finally, if you found this book useful in any way, a review on Amazon is always appreciated!

Made in the USA
Columbia, SC
08 July 2019